Robert Freynet

RED RIVER MISSION

THE STORY OF A PEOPLE AND THEIR CHURCH

VIDACOM

PROLOGUE

IN 1738, THE EXPLORER LAVÉRENDRYE SEEKS A TRANSCONTINENTAL ROUTE TO THE PACIFIC OCEAN. IN THE NAME OF NEW-FRANCE, HE NAVIGATES ENDLESS WATERWAYS TO THE CENTER OF THE NORTH AMERICAN CONTINENT IN A BIRCHBARK CANOE. THE FUR TRADER ARRIVES AT THE FORKS, AT THE CONFLUENCE OF THE RED AND ASSINIBOINE RIVERS, THE TRADITIONAL MEETING PLACE OF FIRST NATIONS. AT THIS STRATEGIC SPOT, HE DECIDES TO ESTABLISH FORT ROUGE.

THE FRENCH-CANADIAN VOYAGEURS SETTLE HERE, AT THIS PLACE CALLED RED RIVER. THEY START FAMILIES, HAVING TAKEN NATIVE WOMEN AS THEIR WIVES. THEIR CHILDREN BECOME THE MÉTIS PEOPLE. SINCE THE EARLY 19TH CENTURY, THESE PROUD FRENCH MÉTIS CALL THEMSELVES THE NEW NATION OF THE WESTERN PRAIRIES. THE FUR TRADE IS THEIR MAIN OCCUPATION.

LORD SELKIRK OF THE HUDSON'S BAY COMPANY HAS A DREAM, THAT OF ESTABLISHING AN AGRICULTURAL COLONY AT RED RIVER, IN THE VERY HEART OF FUR TRADING COUNTRY.

IN THE AUTUMN OF 1812, THIS WEALTHY SCOTSMAN SPONSORS THE IMMIGRATION OF POOR COLONISTS FROM THE BRITISH ISLES, THE MAJORITY FROM SCOTLAND. HOWEVER, THEY ARRIVE UNPREPARED AND UNABLE TO SURVIVE WITHOUT THE HELP OF THE FIRST NATIONS AND THE FRENCH MÉTIS, WHO ARE NATIVE TO THE AREA AND WHO SUPPLY THESE NEWCOMERS WITH FOOD, MOSTLY PEMMICAN, MADE FROM DRIED BISON MEAT.

SELKIRK AND HIS ASSOCIATES BADLY MISMANAGE THE COLONIZATION OF RED RIVER. BECAUSE THE COLONISTS ARE NOT EQUIPPED TO UNDERTAKE AGRICULTURAL ACTIVITIES, FAMINE REARS ITS UGLY HEAD.

EXTREME MEASURES ARE TAKEN IN AN ATTEMPT TO REDRESS THE SITUATION...

* THE BRACKETS < > INDICATE ENGLISH SPEECH OR NATIVE SPEECH. OTHERWISE FRENCH IS SPOKEN.

OCTOBER 1815. THE CHIEF FACTOR OF THE HUDSON'S BAY COMPANY SENDS FOR JEAN-BAPTISTE LAGIMODIÈRE.
< SINCE THE GOVERNOR'S PROCLAMATION FORBIDDING THE SALE OF PEMMICAN OUTSIDE THE COLONY, REBELLION IS IN THE AIR AT RED RIVER ! THE COLONY'S VERY EXISTENCE IS THREATENED ! >
< THE MÉTIS DON'T WANT YOUR COMPANY TO HAVE A MONOPOLY ON TRADE. THEY WANT TO BE ABLE TO SELL THEIR PEMMICAN FREELY. >
< BUT WE NEED TO KEEP ALL THE PEMMICAN WITHIN THE COLONY, TO AVOID A FAMINE. >
< OUR SETTLERS HAVE NO TOOLS TO FARM WITH ! >
< AND HOW IS ANY PEMMICAN TO BE PRODUCED IF THE GOVERNOR FORBIDS THE MÉTIS FROM RIDING THEIR HORSES TO HUNT BISON? >
< WELL, THE COLONISTS DON'T HAVE HORSES ! THANKS TO THEIR MOUNTS, THE MÉTIS HAVE AN UNFAIR ADVANTAGE OVER THE COLONISTS AT THE HUNT ! >
< SIR, THE VIOLENCE HAS TO STOP. THE COLONY IS FAILING ! MY WIFE WANTS TO LEAVE THIS PLACE ! >
< JEAN-BAPTISTE, THIS IS WHY I'VE CALLED YOU HERE. I MUST HAVE A MESSAGE DELIVERED TO LORD SELKIRK TO WARN HIM OF THE GREAT DANGER FACING HIS COLONY. HE MUST SEND US A MILITARY FORCE TO MAINTAIN LAW AND ORDER. >
< CAN I COUNT ON YOU TO DELIVER THIS MESSAGE? I'LL PAY YOU WELL. >
< WHERE IS LORD SELKIRK? >
< IN MONTRÉAL. >
< MONTRÉAL ! >
< I KNOW IT'S FAR... >
< ...AND IT'LL BE WINTER SOON ! >
< THAT JOURNEY WOULD TAKE SEVERAL MONTHS ! MY WIFE, MY CHILDREN... >
< THEY CAN MOVE TO FORT DOUGLAS AND SPEND THE WINTER HERE. >
< WHAT DO YOU SAY? YOU'RE THE BEST MAN FOR THE JOB ! >
< VERY WELL. I ACCEPT. >
< I'LL DELIVER YOUR MESSAGE. >
< HERE. AND BE CAREFUL WITH THIS DOCUMENT. YOU MUST PERSONALLY DELIVER IT TO LORD SELKIRK. >

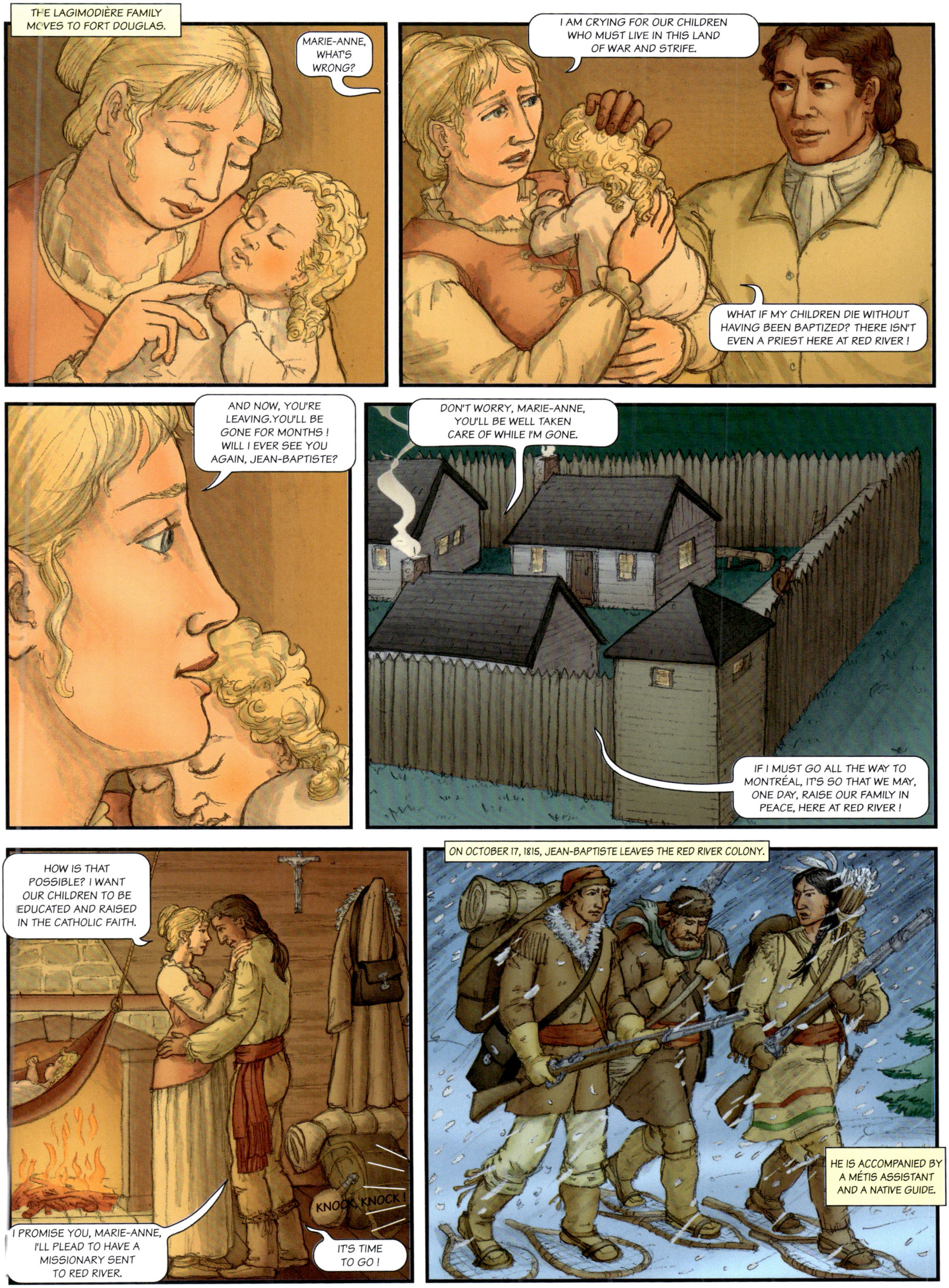
THE LAGIMODIÈRE FAMILY MOVES TO FORT DOUGLAS.
MARIE-ANNE, WHAT'S WRONG?
I AM CRYING FOR OUR CHILDREN WHO MUST LIVE IN THIS LAND OF WAR AND STRIFE.
WHAT IF MY CHILDREN DIE WITHOUT HAVING BEEN BAPTIZED? THERE ISN'T EVEN A PRIEST HERE AT RED RIVER !
AND NOW, YOU'RE LEAVING.YOU'LL BE GONE FOR MONTHS ! WILL I EVER SEE YOU AGAIN, JEAN-BAPTISTE?
DON'T WORRY, MARIE-ANNE, YOU'LL BE WELL TAKEN CARE OF WHILE I'M GONE.
IF I MUST GO ALL THE WAY TO MONTRÉAL, IT'S SO THAT WE MAY, ONE DAY, RAISE OUR FAMILY IN PEACE, HERE AT RED RIVER !
HOW IS THAT POSSIBLE? I WANT OUR CHILDREN TO BE EDUCATED AND RAISED IN THE CATHOLIC FAITH.
I PROMISE YOU, MARIE-ANNE, I'LL PLEAD TO HAVE A MISSIONARY SENT TO RED RIVER.
KNOCK KNOCK !
IT'S TIME TO GO !
ON OCTOBER 17, 1815, JEAN-BAPTISTE LEAVES THE RED RIVER COLONY.
HE IS ACCOMPANIED BY A MÉTIS ASSISTANT AND A NATIVE GUIDE.

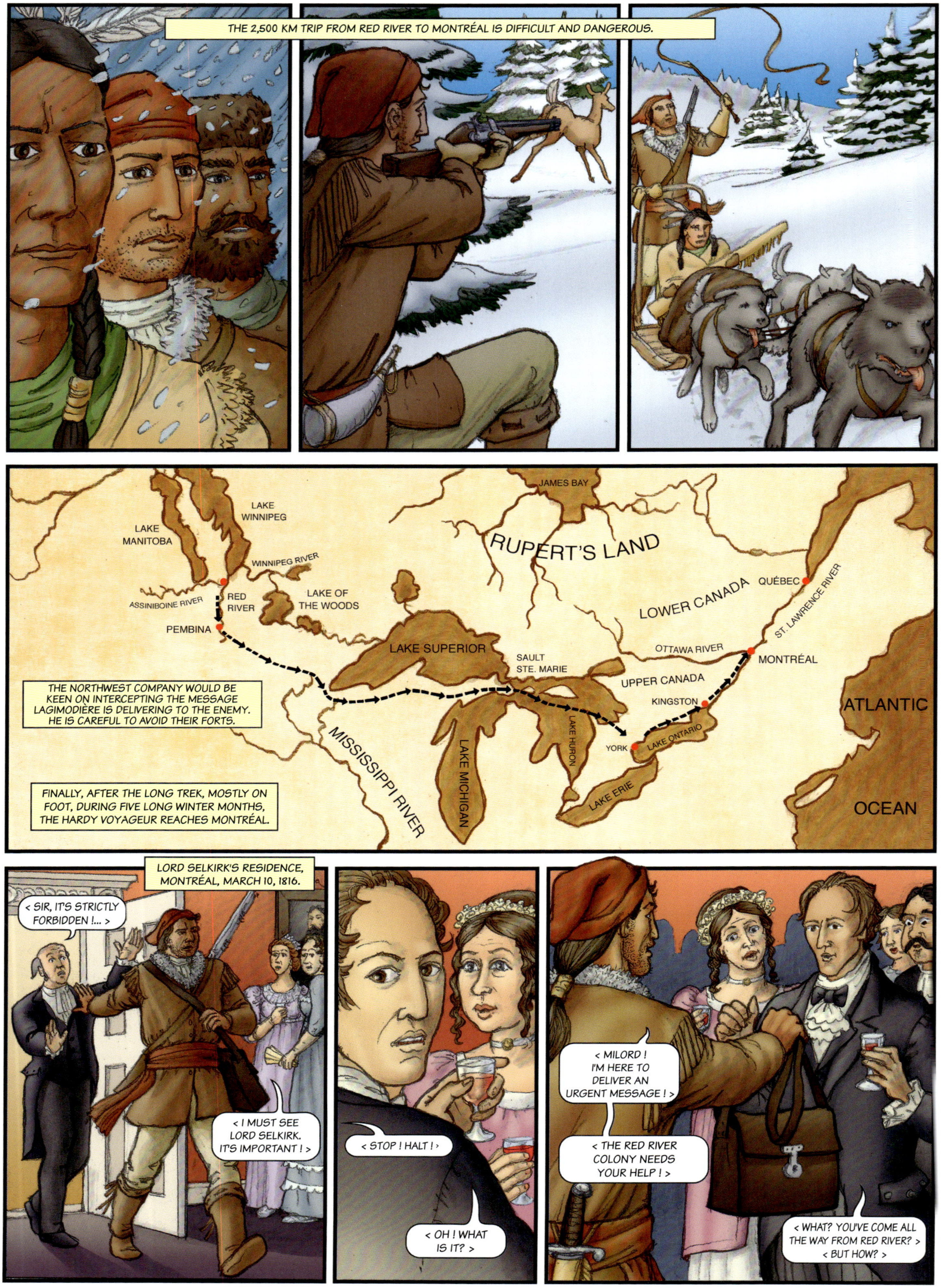
THE 2,500 KM TRIP FROM RED RIVER TO MONTRÉAL IS DIFFICULT AND DANGEROUS.
JAMES BAY
LAKE WINNIPEG
LAKE MANITOBA
RUPERT'S LAND
WINNIPEG RIVER
QUÉBEC
ASSINIBOINE RIVER
RED RIVER
LAKE OF THE WOODS
LOWER CANADA
ST. LAWRENCE RIVER
PEMBINA
LAKE SUPERIOR
SAULT STE. MARIE
OTTAWA RIVER
MONTRÉAL
UPPER CANADA
KINGSTON
ATLANTIC
THE NORTHWEST COMPANY WOULD BE KEEN ON INTERCEPTING THE MESSAGE LAGIMODIÈRE IS DELIVERING TO THE ENEMY. HE IS CAREFUL TO AVOID THEIR FORTS.
MISSISSIPPI RIVER
LAKE MICHIGAN
LAKE HURON
YORK
LAKE ONTARIO
LAKE ERIE
OCEAN
FINALLY, AFTER THE LONG TREK, MOSTLY ON FOOT, DURING FIVE LONG WINTER MONTHS, THE HARDY VOYAGEUR REACHES MONTRÉAL.
LORD SELKIRK'S RESIDENCE, MONTRÉAL, MARCH 10, 1816.
< SIR, IT'S STRICTLY FORBIDDEN !... >
< I MUST SEE LORD SELKIRK. IT'S IMPORTANT ! >
< STOP ! HALT ! >
< OH ! WHAT IS IT? >
< MILORD ! I'M HERE TO DELIVER AN URGENT MESSAGE ! >
< THE RED RIVER COLONY NEEDS YOUR HELP ! >
< WHAT? YOU'VE COME ALL THE WAY FROM RED RIVER? >
< BUT HOW? >

A LITTLE LATER...
< HMMM...THE COLONY SURVIVES STILL, BUT THERE'S A REBELLION BREWING THAT MAY DESTROY IT ! >
< AN ARMED FORCE WILL BE NEEDED TO RE-ESTABLISH PEACE AND ORDER ! >
< JEAN-BAPTISTE LAGIMODIÈRE, YOU'VE DELIVERED A VERY IMPORTANT MESSAGE. YOUR JOURNEY IN THE DEAD OF WINTER WAS, NO DOUBT, PERILOUS ! >
< I ADMIRE YOU AND AM GRATEFUL TO YOU FOR HAVING CARRIED OUT THIS EXTRAORDINARY FEAT ! >
< ASK ME ANYTHING IN RETURN AND I SHALL GIVE IT TO YOU ! >
< PRIESTS ! >
< PARDON ME? >
< SEND CATHOLIC PRIESTS TO THE RED RIVER SETTLEMENT ! >
ON JUNE 19, 1816, BACK AT THE COLONY, IN A PLACE CALLED SEVEN OAKS, A BATTLE ERUPTS BETWEEN MÉTIS FROM THE NORTHWEST COMPANY AND THE ENGLISH EMPLOYEES OF THE HUDSON'S BAY COMPANY.
DURING THE BATTLE OF SEVEN OAKS, 21 ENGLISH COMBATANTS, AS WELL AS GOVERNOR SEMPLE, ARE KILLED. THE MÉTIS LOSE ONE OF THEIR OWN.
IT IS NOW OPEN WARFARE AT RED RIVER.
LORD SELKIRK HIRES 74 MOSTLY SWISS MERCENARIES—THE DE MEURONS REGIMENT.
HE MAKES HIS WAY, WITH HIS SMALL ARMY, TOWARDS RED RIVER.
LAGIMODIÈRE ALSO RETURNS TO THE COLONY. HE FINALLY ARRIVES HOME AT CHRISTMASTIME, 1816.
THE DE MEURONS REGIMENT REACHES THE FORKS ON JANUARY 10, 1817.
THE REGIMENT CAPTURES FORT GIBRALTAR WHICH BELONGS TO THE NORTHWEST COMPANY.

LORD SELKIRK TAKES BACK CONTROL OF THE COLONY. HE NEGOTIATES TREATIES WITH THE FIRST NATIONS PEOPLES. HE DRAWS PLANS FOR THE CONSTRUCTION OF ROADS AND THE DISTRIBUTION OF LOTS.
‹ HERE, ON THE RIVER SHORE OPPOSITE THE FORKS WILL BE THE LOCATION OF THE CATHOLIC MISSION. ›
‹ A CATHOLIC MISSION MILORD? ›
‹ YES, I PROMISED LAGIMODIÈRE SOME PRIESTS FOR RED RIVER. I SHALL HONOUR MY PROMISE. ›
‹ GOD KNOWS THAT RELIGION WILL HELP TO PACIFY THIS TROUBLED LAND ! ›
‹ I'VE ALREADY ASKED THE BISHOP OF QUÉBEC TO SEND MISSIONARIES. ›
AT QUÉBEC, BISHOP PLESSIS RECEIVES THE REQUEST.
HMMM... LORD SELKIRK—A PROTESTANT—IS ASKING THAT CATHOLIC MISSIONARIES BE SENT TO HIS COLONY AT THE RED RIVER !
HE'S EVEN OFFERING A LARGE PIECE OF LAND WHERE WE COULD ESTABLISH A MISSION !
THIS IS GOOD NEWS, YOUR EXCELLENCY !
THE MÉTIS POPULATION THERE IS OF FRENCH DESCENT AND THEY ARE BELIEVERS. THEY'VE BEEN ASKING FOR MISSIONARIES.
YES, LET US BRING THE GOSPEL TO THAT FARAWAY LAND.
BUT WHO SHOULD WE SEND?
SOON AT KAMOURASKA, IN LOWER CANADA...
PASTOR, A LETTER FROM OUR BISHOP !
HE'S ASKING YOU TO GO ON A MISSION TO THE NORTHWEST, TO RED RIVER !
ME? A MISSIONARY?
JOSEPH-NORBERT PROVENCHER, A 33-YEAR OLD PRIEST, DELIBERATES THE REQUEST FOR A LONG TIME BEFORE FINALLY ANSWERING.
A SAINT FRANCIS OR A SAINT BONIFACE WOULD BE MORE FITTING TO PREACH THE WORD OF GOD IN THIS VAST, FARAWAY LAND. BUT...
MAY PROVIDENCE NOW DECIDE UPON MY DESTINY. I SHALL OBEY.
ON MAY 19, 1818, FATHER PROVENCHER LEAVES MONTRÉAL IN THE COMPANY OF FATHER SÉVÈRE DUMOULIN AND OF A SEMINARIAN, IN ORDER TO FOUND A MISSION AT RED RIVER, SEVERAL THOUSAND KILOMETERS AWAY, IN THE GREAT NORTHWEST.

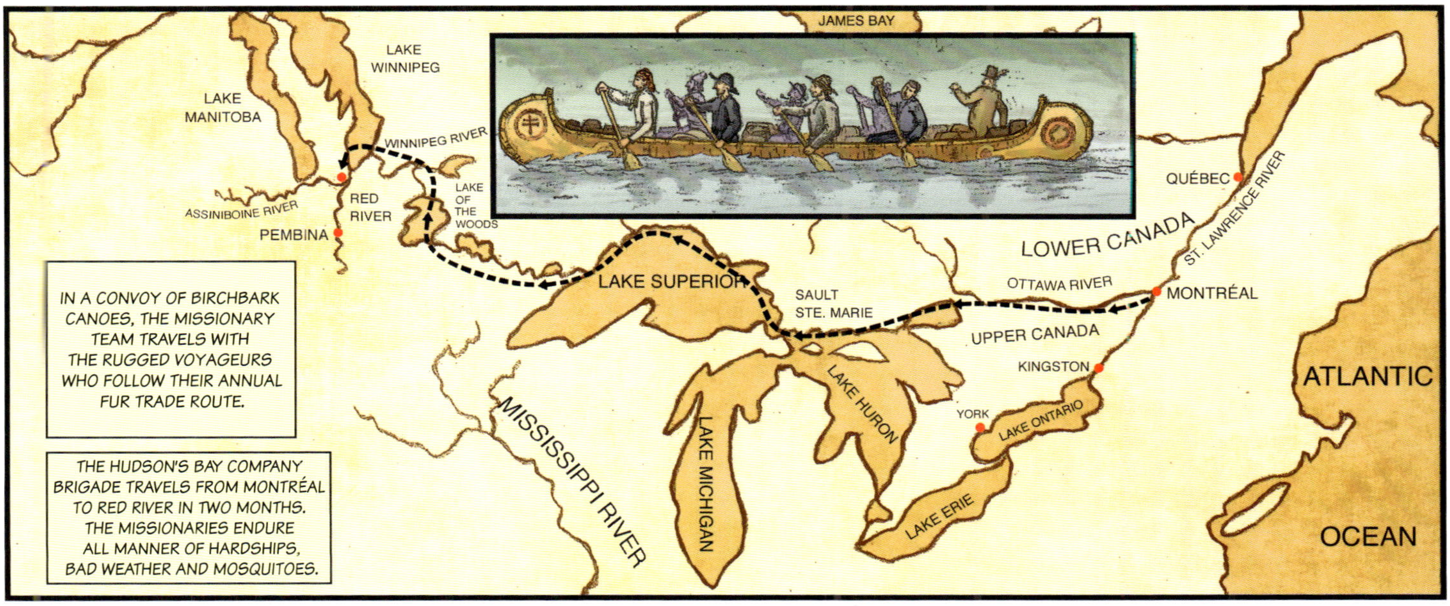
JAMES BAY
LAKE WINNIPEG
LAKE MANITOBA
WINNIPEG RIVER
ASSINIBOINE RIVER
RED RIVER
PEMBINA
LAKE OF THE WOODS
QUÉBEC
ST. LAWRENCE RIVER
LOWER CANADA
OTTAWA RIVER
MONTRÉAL
LAKE SUPERIOR
SAULT STE. MARIE
UPPER CANADA
KINGSTON
ATLANTIC
OCEAN
LAKE HURON
LAKE MICHIGAN
MISSISSIPPI RIVER
YORK
LAKE ONTARIO
LAKE ERIE
IN A CONVOY OF BIRCHBARK CANOES, THE MISSIONARY TEAM TRAVELS WITH THE RUGGED VOYAGEURS WHO FOLLOW THEIR ANNUAL FUR TRADE ROUTE.
THE HUDSON'S BAY COMPANY BRIGADE TRAVELS FROM MONTRÉAL TO RED RIVER IN TWO MONTHS. THE MISSIONARIES ENDURE ALL MANNER OF HARDSHIPS, BAD WEATHER AND MOSQUITOES.

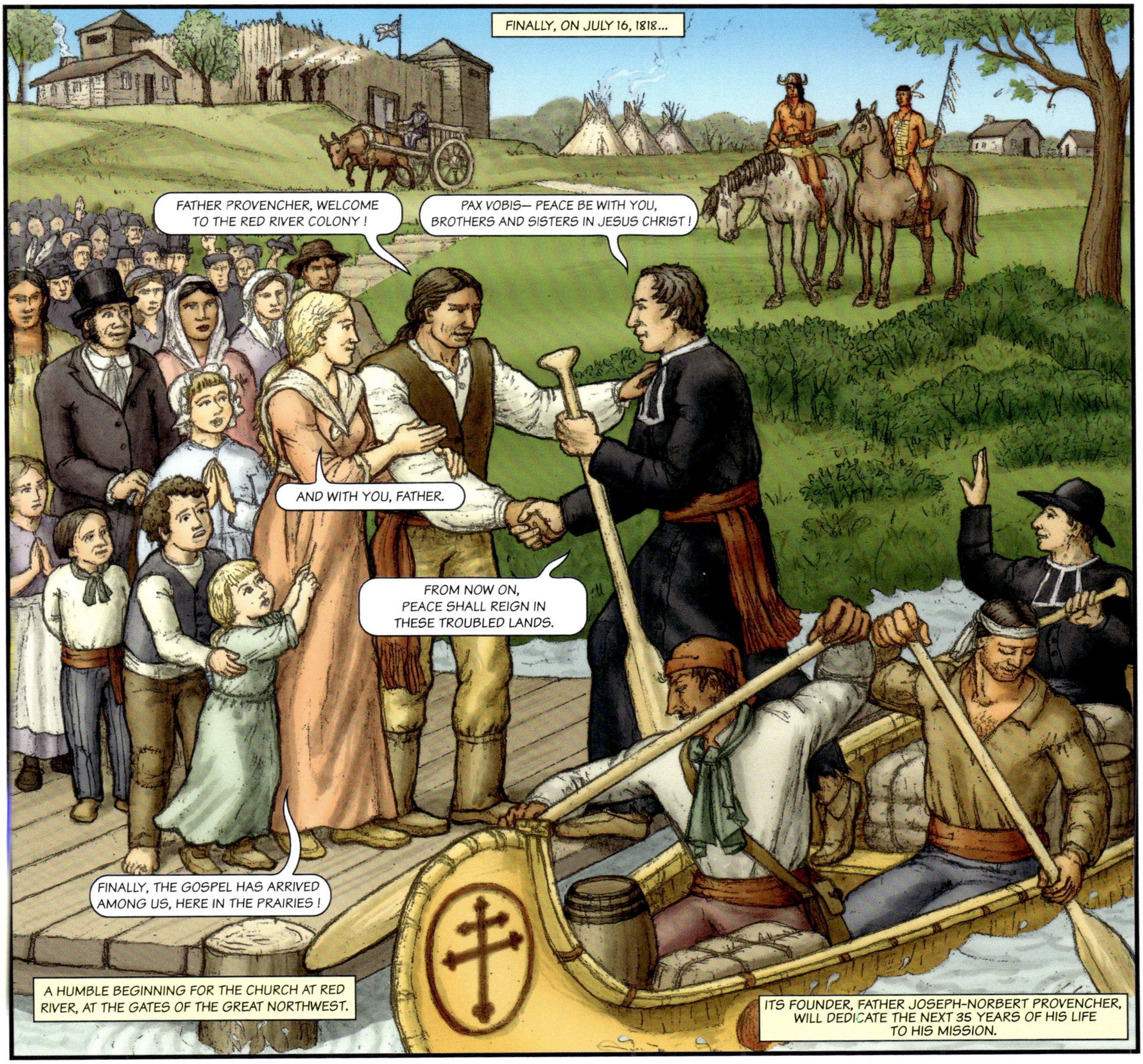
FINALLY, ON JULY 16, 1818...
FATHER PROVENCHER, WELCOME TO THE RED RIVER COLONY !
PAX VOBIS— PEACE BE WITH YOU, BROTHERS AND SISTERS IN JESUS CHRIST !
AND WITH YOU, FATHER.
FROM NOW ON, PEACE SHALL REIGN IN THESE TROUBLED LANDS.
FINALLY, THE GOSPEL HAS ARRIVED AMONG US, HERE IN THE PRAIRIES !
A HUMBLE BEGINNING FOR THE CHURCH AT RED RIVER, AT THE GATES OF THE GREAT NORTHWEST.
ITS FOUNDER, FATHER JOSEPH-NORBERT PROVENCHER, WILL DEDICATE THE NEXT 35 YEARS OF HIS LIFE TO HIS MISSION.

< FATHER PROVENCHER, AS GOVERNOR OF THIS COLONY, IT IS MY HONOUR TO WELCOME YOU TO FORT DOUGLAS. >
< THANK YOU MR. MCDONNELL. >
< I CAN OFFER YOU QUARTERS AT THE FORT. >
< IN FACT, I WAS THINKING OF ORGANIZING A BAPTISM CEREMONY FOR TOMORROW. >
SOON, AT FORT DOUGLAS...
MARIE-ANNE, COULD YOU MAKE SURE THAT ALL THE MOTHERS IN THE COLONY BRING THEIR CHILDREN FIVE YEARS OLD AND YOUNGER TO THE FORT TOMORROW, SO THAT THEY MAY BE BAPTIZED?
VERY WELL, FATHER.
MAY I ALSO ASK THAT YOU SERVE AS THEIR GODMOTHER?
OF ALL THE CHILDREN?
WELL, MARIE-ANNE, YOU ARE IN FACT THE ONLY BAPTIZED CATHOLIC WOMAN IN THE AREA
ON JULY 17, 1818.
EGO TE BAPTIZO IN NOMINE PATRIS ET FILII ET SPIRITUS SANCTI.
MARIE-ANNE LAGIMODIÈRE BECOMES GODMOTHER TO MORE THAN 100 CHILDREN.
EVER SINCE THAT DAY, THE CHILDREN OF RED RIVER USE THE TERM OF ENDEARMENT "MA MARRAINE" (MY GODMOTHER) FOR HER.
ON THE FOLLOWING DAY, A SUNDAY, FATHER PROVENCHER CELEBRATES THE FIRST MASS AT RED RIVER.
... HOC EST ENIM CORPUS MEUM.
THE ZEALOUS MISSIONARIES TEACH CATECHISM EVERY DAY TO THE BOYS AND GIRLS OF THE COLONY.
SOON, JEAN-BAPTISTE LAGIMODIÈRE ACCOMPANIES FATHER PROVENCHER TO THE PARCEL OF LAND THAT LORD SELKIRK GRANTED TO THE CATHOLIC MISSION.
HERE WE ARE FATHER, ON THE BANKS OF THE RED RIVER.
ACROSS THE WATER IS FORT GIBRALTAR, ON THE BANK OF THE ASSINIBOINE RIVER, WHICH STRETCHES OUT TO THE WEST.
THIS CONFLUENCE OF RIVERS IS CALLED THE FORKS.
LIKE THE RAYS OF THE SETTING SUN, THE GOSPEL MUST SHINE ON THIS VAST LAND TO THE WEST.

THE CLERGYMEN GET TO WORK BUILDING, ON THEIR LAND, A CHAPEL WITH ONE ROOM— THEIR FIRST RESIDENCE.
TCHAC !
PROVENCHER WORKS HARD AS A LUMBER-JACK, A LABOURER, A CARPENTER, A MASON.
DESPITE THE LACK OF MEANS AND MATERIALS, THEY MANAGE TO PUT UP A HUMBLE CABIN BEFORE WINTER.
PROVENCHER'S CHAPEL IS THE FIRST PERMANENT CATHOLIC MISSION IN THE WEST.
THE CHAPEL IS CONSECRATED ON ALL SAINTS DAY, NOVEMBER 1, 1818, UNDER THE NAME OF SAINT BONIFACE, A GREAT EUROPEAN MISSIONARY OF THE EIGHTH CENTURY.
... SANCTE BONIFACII MARTYRIS TUI ATQUE PONTIFICIS INTERCESSIO GLORIOSA NOS PROTEGAT.
ON THIS OCCASION, REINE AND LAPRAIRIE LAGIMODIÈRE, THE ELDEST CHILDREN OF JEAN-BAPTISTE AND MARIE-ANNE, RECEIVE THEIR FIRST COMMUNION.
IN 1821, IN MONTRÉAL, THE ENGLISH SHAREHOLDERS OF THE TWO COMPANIES—THE HUDSON'S BAY COMPANY AND THE NORTHWEST COMPANY—MERGE THEIR INTERESTS, EFFECTIVELY ELIMINATING ALL COMPETITION.
< THANKS TO OUR MONOPOLY, DEAR PARTNER, I SEE PROFITS ON THE HORIZON ! >
< WE ARE THE CAESARS OF THIS TERRITORY, AS VAST AS ALL OF EUROPE ! >
PRO PELLE CUTEM
HBC
NWC°
THE NEW CORPORATION RETAINS THE NAME OF THE HUDSON'S BAY COMPANY.
AT LAST, THE RED RIVER COLONY CAN GROW AND PROSPER IN PEACE.
HOWEVER, THE INHABITANTS ARE PUT TO THE TEST IN THE FIRST YEARS. THEY MUST ENDURE DROUGHTS, FLOODS, KILLER FROSTS AND GRASSHOPPERS.

WINTER APPROACHES...
PASTOR, MOST OF THE MÉTIS AND SETTLERS ARE DESERTING THE COLONY TO GO SOUTH TO PEMBINA.
WE CAN'T BLAME THEM ! HERE AT RED RIVER, FOOD IS SCARCE IN THE WINTER.
BUT OVER THERE, IN THE LAND OF THE BISON, THEY CAN BETTER SURVIVE THE RIGOURS OF WINTER.
WILL WE STAY HERE?
NO. THE SHEPHERD MUST FOLLOW HIS FLOCK. YOU'LL MINISTER TO THE MÉTIS AND EDUCATE THE BOYS.
THUS, FATHER DUMOULIN AND THE SEMINARIAN SPEND THE WINTER AT PEMBINA, 110 KM SOUTH OF THE FORKS, WITH THE MÉTIS FAMILIES AND ENGLISH SETTLERS.
DUMOULIN OPENS A SCHOOL FOR BOYS, WITH OVER 60 STUDENTS ENROLLED.
AS FOR PROVENCHER, HE ALSO FOUNDS, IN 1818, A SCHOOL FOR BOYS, THIS ONE AT RED RIVER, TO TEACH THE RUDIMENTS OF READING AND WRITING.
ABC
DEF
GHI
SOON...
FATHER, REINE WOULD LIKE TO ASK YOU SOMETHING...
YES?
I TOO WOULD LIKE TO LEARN TO READ AND WRITE, LIKE MY BROTHER. WILL THERE BE A SCHOOL FOR GIRLS?
LET'S PRAY THAT I'LL BE ABLE TO FIND AN ORDER OF NUNS WHO WILL COME TO TEACH THE GIRLS AT RED RIVER.
THERE IS MUCH POVERTY IN THE COLONY. ONE DAY, AS THE CATECHISM CLASS IS DISMISSED...
REINE, ONE MINUTE PLEASE.
YES?
LISTEN, REINE. TELL YOUR MOTHER THAT I HAVEN'T ANYTHING TO EAT THIS EVENING.
VERY WELL, FATHER.
AND SOON...
HERE, FATHER, A BAG OF PEMMICAN FOR YOU.
AH, THANK YOU, REINE. AND THANK YOUR MOTHER FOR ME.
ALSO, MOTHER SENDS YOU A SURPRISE !
A SURPRISE?
MILK ! BUT...HOW?
OUR COW HAS STARTED GIVING MILK !
WHAT A LUXURY !

END OF OCTOBER, 1820, BISHOP'S PALACE, QUÉBEC.
MONSEIGNEUR PLESSIS, AS AGREED, I'VE COME TO REPORT ON THE FIRST TWO YEARS OF THE MISSION YOU HAVE ENTRUSTED ME WITH AT RED RIVER.
WHAT A VALIANT MISSIONARY YOU ARE, FATHER PROVENCHER, AND IN SUCH A DISTANT LAND !
YOU, WHO WORKS SO HARD TO ESTABLISH A SOLID BASE FOR THE CHURCH IN THE WEST. TELL ME EVERYTHING—I AM LISTENING, MY SON !
AND LATER...
I'VE JUST COME BACK FROM ROME AND LONDON.
I'VE MANAGED TO HAVE MY VAST DIOCESE PARTITIONED.
I WANT TO CREATE A NEW DIOCESE TO THE NORTH-WEST OF LAKE SUPERIOR, UP TO THE FOOT OF THE ROCKY MOUNTAINS AND INCLUDING THE ARCTIC.
CERTAINLY AN IMMENSE TERRITORY !
AND BECAUSE THIS DOCUMENT, SIGNED BY HIS HOLINESS THE POPE HIMSELF, BEARS YOUR NAME, I PRESENT IT TO YOU.
WHAT IS IT?
IT'S THE DECREE NAMING YOU TITULAR BISHOP OF JULIOPOLIS FOR THE NORTHWEST AND COADJUTOR TO MYSELF, BISHOP OF QUÉBEC.
YOUR GRACE, I MUST RETURN THIS DECREE TO YOU.
Y-YOU REFUSE THE NOMINATION?
I TREMBLE AT THE VERY IDEA OF BEING ELEVATED TO THE RANK OF BISHOP. THE RESPONSIBILITY IS TOO GREAT !
I'LL HAVE TO REFLECT UPON THIS.
PROVENCHER FINALLY ACQUIESCES TO BISHOP PLESSIS' WISH.
ON MAY 12, 1822, AT TROIS-RIVIÈRES, THREE BISHOPS CONFER UPON HIM THE EPISCOPAL CONSECRATION.
HE THUS BECOMES THE CATHOLIC PASTOR FOR THE MANY SOULS INHABITING A GREAT EXPANSE IN BRITISH NORTH AMERICA.
PACIFIC OCEAN
ROCKY MOUNTAINS
ARCTIC ARCHIPELAGO
HUDSON BAY
JAMES BAY
RUPERT'S LAND
UNITED STATES
UPPER CANADA
AFTER TWO YEARS SPENT IN LOWER CANADA, PROVENCHER RETURNS TO RED RIVER AS A CONSECRATED BISHOP.

BISHOP JOSEPH-NORBERT PROVENCHER WORKS HARD TO ESTABLISH HIS DIOCESE.
DESPITE HIS ELEVATED TITLE, HE DOESN'T SHUN GRUELING FARM LABOUR IN ORDER TO SURVIVE IN THIS UNTAMED LAND.
THROUGH EXAMPLE, THIS BISHOP OF IMPOSING BUILD AND HERCULEAN STRENGTH WISHES TO DRAW THE NOMADIC MÉTIS INTO A MORE SEDENTARY AND AGRICULTURAL WAY OF LIFE.
HE MEETS WITH THE NEW GOVERNOR OF THE COLONY, GEORGE SIMPSON.
< SIR, I'VE DECIDED TO START THE CONSTRUCTION OF A STONE CATHEDRAL. >
< OF COURSE, YOUR GRACE. A CATHEDRAL FOR THE NEW DIOCESE... >
< I WOULD BE HAPPY TO OFFER, IN THE NAME OF THE COMPANY, 100 POUNDS STERLING TO HELP GET YOUR PROJECT OFF THE GROUND. >
< A CATHEDRAL...HERE AT RED RIVER. THAT WOULD BE GOOD FOR THE COLONY ! >
PROVENCHER RAISES FUNDS LOCALLY, AS WELL AS IN LOWER CANADA AND IN FRANCE. HE MANAGES TO ERECT AN IMPOSING CATHEDRAL MADE OF FIELD STONES, ON THE BANKS OF THE RED RIVER, OPPOSITE THE FORKS.
HE BRINGS IN SKILLED WORKERS FROM THE EAST.
THE MASON AND LEGENDARY STRONGMAN VOYAGEUR, JEAN-BAPTISTE CHARBONNEAU, IS ONE OF THE WORKERS.
HEY, CHARBONNEAU ! CAN YOU CARRY THIS ROCK OVER THERE?
ARE YOU CRAZY? WHO COULD EVER CARRY THAT ALONE?
LET ME DO THAT !
NOW THAT'S A JOB FOR A MAN !
WHAT DID YOU SAY?
YOU DON'T THINK I'M A MAN?

WE'LL SEE WHO'S A MAN HERE !
CHARBONNEAU, WHAT ARE YOU DOING?
ARE YOU GOING TO FIGHT WITH YOUR BISHOP?
HUH?...MY BISHOP...UH...
EXCUSE ME YOUR GRACE !
I FORGOT...
I FORGIVE YOU FOR YOUR BAD TEMPER, MY SON.
IN 1831, FATHER GEORGES-ANTOINE BELCOURT ARRIVES AT RED RIVER. HE QUICKLY LEARNS THE SAULTEAUX LANGUAGE.
HE TRIES TO EVANGELIZE A NOMADIC TRIBE IN A MISSION HE FOUNDS ALONG THE ASSINIBOINE RIVER.
HOW AM I SUPPOSED TO TEACH RELIGION IN A CONTINUOUS WAY TO A PEOPLE ALWAYS ON THE MOVE?
< BROTHERS, SISTERS, LET US REMAIN HERE TO CULTIVATE THE LAND. >
< WE'LL BE ABLE TO SOW AND HARVEST OUR OWN FOOD HERE, AND NOT HAVE TO DEPEND ONLY ON HUNTING. >
< BLACK ROBE ! >
< YES, CHIEF PEGUIS. >
< BEFORE THE WHITE PEOPLE CAME AND TROUBLED OUR LAND, OUR RIVERS WERE FULL OF FISH, AND DEER WERE PLENTIFUL IN OUR FORESTS ! >
< YOU FURROW THE EARTH WITH YOUR PLOWS, COVERING THE PRAIRIES WITH COWS IN THE SUMMER AND FEEDING YOUR ANIMALS IN THE WINTER WITH HAY CUT FROM OUR BISON'S PASTURES. >
< WITHOUT THE BISON, WE WILL BE REDUCED TO POVERTY ! >
BISHOP PROVENCHER SUMMONS FATHER BELCOURT...
I'M WORRIED ABOUT ALL THE COSTS OF YOUR VARIOUS MISSIONS: BUILDINGS, TOOLS, MATERIALS, WORKERS...
BUT YOUR GRACE, WE NEED THOSE FACILITIES TO ENCOURAGE THE NATIVE TRIBES TO SETTLE DOWN IN A SPECIFIC AREA AND START FARMING.
IT'S ALMOST IMPOSSIBLE TO EFFECTIVELY TEACH CHRISTIAN DOCTRINE TO A TRIBE OF NOMADIC HUNTERS !

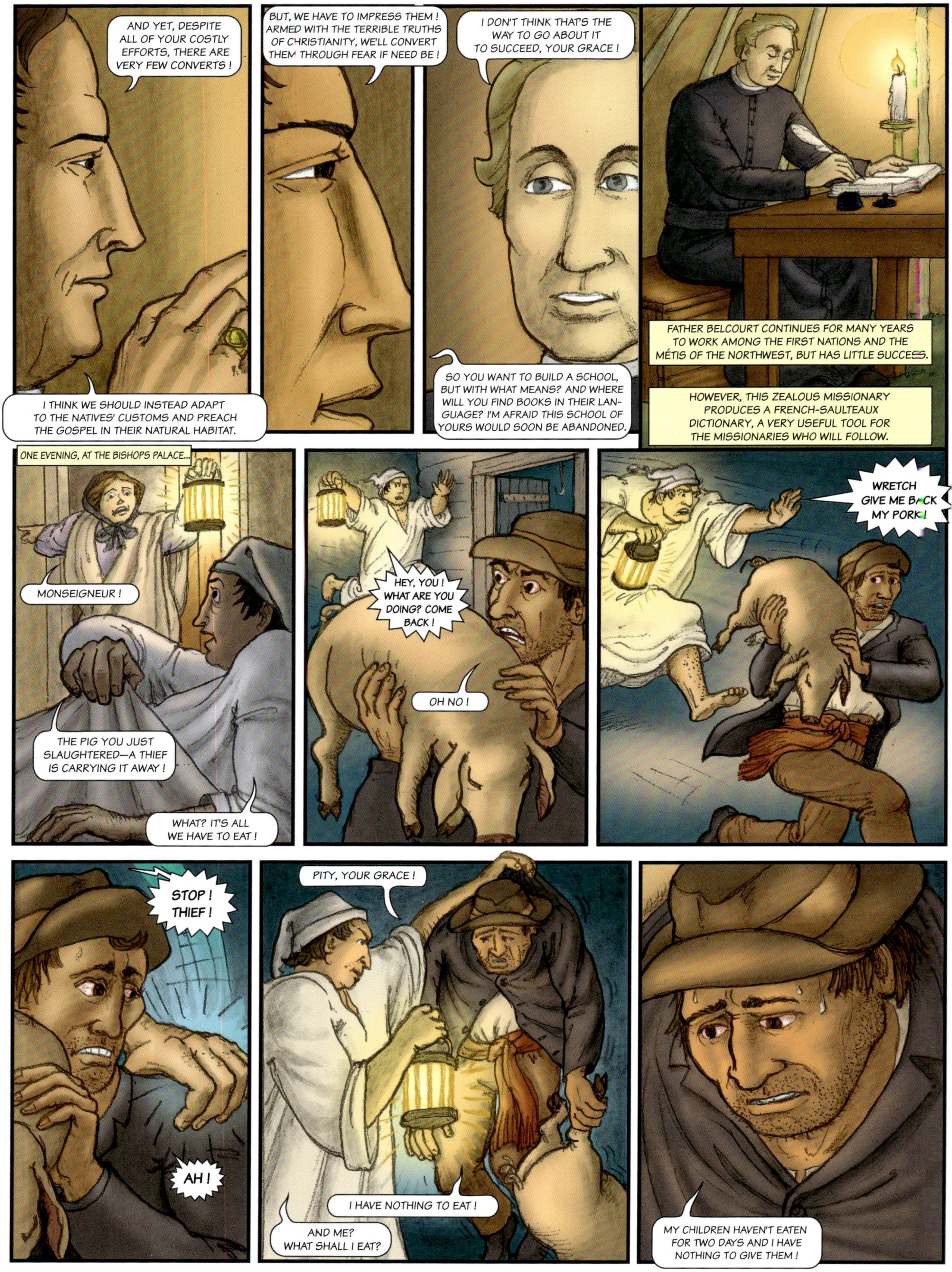
AND YET, DESPITE ALL OF YOUR COSTLY EFFORTS, THERE ARE VERY FEW CONVERTS !
I THINK WE SHOULD INSTEAD ADAPT TO THE NATIVES' CUSTOMS AND PREACH THE GOSPEL IN THEIR NATURAL HABITAT.
BUT, WE HAVE TO IMPRESS THEM ! ARMED WITH THE TERRIBLE TRUTHS OF CHRISTIANITY, WE'LL CONVERT THEM THROUGH FEAR IF NEED BE !
I DON'T THINK THAT'S THE WAY TO GO ABOUT IT TO SUCCEED, YOUR GRACE !
SO YOU WANT TO BUILD A SCHOOL, BUT WITH WHAT MEANS? AND WHERE WILL YOU FIND BOOKS IN THEIR LANGUAGE? I'M AFRAID THIS SCHOOL OF YOURS WOULD SOON BE ABANDONED.
FATHER BELCOURT CONTINUES FOR MANY YEARS TO WORK AMONG THE FIRST NATIONS AND THE MÉTIS OF THE NORTHWEST, BUT HAS LITTLE SUCCESS.
HOWEVER, THIS ZEALOUS MISSIONARY PRODUCES A FRENCH-SAULTEAUX DICTIONARY, A VERY USEFUL TOOL FOR THE MISSIONARIES WHO WILL FOLLOW.
ONE EVENING, AT THE BISHOPS PALACE...
MONSEIGNEUR !
THE PIG YOU JUST SLAUGHTERED—A THIEF IS CARRYING IT AWAY !
WHAT? IT'S ALL WE HAVE TO EAT !
HEY, YOU ! WHAT ARE YOU DOING? COME BACK !
OH NO !
WRETCH GIVE ME BACK MY PORK !
STOP ! THIEF !
AH !
PITY, YOUR GRACE !
I HAVE NOTHING TO EAT !
AND ME? WHAT SHALL I EAT?
MY CHILDREN HAVEN'T EATEN FOR TWO DAYS AND I HAVE NOTHING TO GIVE THEM !

YOU SHOULDN'T STEAL !
BRING THIS MEAT BACK TO THE SHED...
...I'LL GIVE YOU HALF OF IT.
THAT WAY, WE'LL BOTH HAVE SOMETHING TO EAT.
AND LATER...
HERE, AND NO MORE STEALING !
ER...TH-THANK YOU, YOUR GRACE !
THE DIOCESE CONTINUES TO GROW. BISHOP PROVENCHER GOES TO MONTRÉAL AND REQUESTS THE SERVICES OF THE GREY NUNS FOR HIS YOUNG DIOCESE AT RED RIVER. HE WANTS THEM TO OPEN A SCHOOL FOR GIRLS AND TO DEDICATE THEMSELVES TO CHARITABLE WORKS.
ON MAY 24, 1844, FOUR BRAVE SISTERS OF CHARITY EMBARK A GIANT BIRCHBARK CANOE ALONG WITH THE VOYAGEURS OF THE HUDSON'S BAY COMPANY, AND LEAVE LACHINE, NEAR MONTRÉAL.
BON VOYAGE, DEAR SISTERS ! BE WITNESSES TO THE LOVE OF GOD AMONG THE POOR.
GENTLEMEN, TAKE GOOD CARE OF MY SISTERS ! ESPECIALLY, NO SWEARING IN THEIR PRESENCE !
YOU HAVE MY WORD, MOTHER SUPERIOR !
PROVENCHER ALSO HEADS BACK TO RED RIVER, IN THE COMPANY OF GOVERNOR SIMPSON, IN HIS EXPRESS CANOE.
OUR MISSION IS TO TEACH AND TO HELP THE POOR AND THE SICK.
IS EVERYONE CATHOLIC AT RED RIVER?
MOST ARE, YES—THE FRENCH MÉTIS, THE SCOTS, THE IRISH—BUT WE WILL BE HELPING EVERYONE.
LIKE THE VOYAGEURS, SISTERS VALADE, LAGRAVE, COUTLÉE AND LAFRANCE ENDURE A DIFFICULT JOURNEY—LONG HOURS IN THE CANOE, RUGGED PORTAGES AND MOSQUITOES...
ON THE WAY, SISTER LAGRAVE SPRAINS HER ANKLE. TWO STRONG IROQUOIS ARE HIRED TO CARRY THE PORTLY NUN DURING THE MANY PORTAGES.
FINALLY, ON JUNE 21, 1844, IN THE MIDDLE OF THE NIGHT, AFTER A 58-DAY VOYAGE BY CANOE, THE GREY NUNS ARE WELCOMED AT RED RIVER BY BISHOP PROVENCHER.

ON JULY 2, 1844, THE SISTERS OF CHARITY OF MONTRÉAL MOVE INTO PROVENCHER'S OLD PRESBYTERY.
THEY WORK HARD AT RESTORING THE BUILDING: REPAIRING, PATCHING, CLEANING.
SOON, ON JULY 17, 1844, IN THE FIRST CONVENT AT RED RIVER, A SCHOOL FOR GIRLS OPENS ITS DOORS AND 27 MÉTIS, SAULTEAUX AND SIOUX GIRLS ARE ENROLLED.
1 2 3 4 5
6 7 8 9 10
A B C D E F G
A WEEK LATER, THE NUNS OPEN A CLASS FOR 43 BOYS ON THE MAIN FLOOR OF THE BISHOP'S HOUSE.
THESE WOMEN PRIESTS KNOW HOW TO TEACH OUR CHILDREN WELL.
YES, THEY TEACH THEM TO READ, TO WRITE, AND TO PRAY THE GREAT MANITOU.
ONE DAY, IN THE GARDEN...
BZZZ
I CAN HARDLY SEE THROUGH THIS CLOUD OF MOSQUITOES !
BZZZ
MY GOD ! SPARE US FROM THIS PLAGUE !
ARE THE MOSQUITOES TROUBLING YOU, DEAR SISTERS?
YOUR GRACE, SURELY GOD WILL ANSWER YOUR PRAYERS ! ASK HIM TO CHASE THEM AWAY !
BZZZ
BZZZ
WORK, DEAR CHILDREN, WORK ! THE LORD WILL HAVE PITY ON YOU.
WHILE CONTINUING HIS WALK, THE PRELATE STARTS TO PRAY THE ROSARY.
OUR FATHER WHO ART IN HEAVEN...
SUDDENLY...
SISTER VALADE ! A BREEZE ! A LOVELY BREEZE IS BLOWING AWAY THE MOSQUITOES !
OH, DELIVERANCE !
I BELIEVE THE LORD ANSWERS THE PRAYERS OF THAT HOLY MAN

SOON, SISTER LAGRAVE, WHOM BISHOP PROVENCHER NICKNAMES HIS "GOOD VICAR", BEGINS TRAVELING TWICE A WEEK TO RIVIÈRE LASALLE (ST. NORBERT), 15 KM SOUTH OF ST. BONIFACE.
SHE TEACHES CATECHISM TO ADULTS AND CHILDREN.
SHE ALSO VISITS THE SICK AND THE POOR IN THE AREA.
HERE, JEAN, TRY TO SWALLOW.
ONE DAY, AT THE CATHEDRAL...
SISTER LAGRAVE, YOU SING HYMNS, AND YOU HAVE GREAT ARTISTIC ABILITIES: YOU MUST FIND MY CATHEDRAL VERY SAD INDEED.
JUST LOOK AT THESE BIG EMPTY WALLS !
IF YOU WISH, I COULD DECORATE THEM.
YES, OF COURSE, THANK YOU ! IN THE TEMPLE OF GOD, TRUTH SHOULD BE EXPRESSED THROUGH BEAUTY.
THE ARTISTIC NUN PROMPTLY BEGINS TO PAINT ON THE WALLS OF THE CATHEDRAL.
THE LADIES OF THE PARISH STAY FOR HOURS, WATCHING SISTER LAGRAVE PAINT !
WHAT FASCINATES THEM SO MUCH?
HER MAGNIFICENT FLORAL MOTIFS !
THE MÉTIS WOMEN NOTE EACH DETAIL AND REPRODUCE THEM IN THEIR BEADWORK.
THE WALLS OF THE CHURCH HAVING BEEN BEAUTIFIED, THERE IS STILL AN IMPORTANT ELEMENT MISSING FROM THE DECOR...
THE TALENTED SISTER LAGRAVE GETS TO WORK.
SOON, SHE CREATES A LOVELY STATUE OF THE VIRGIN MARY, IN PAPIER-MÂCHÉ, INVITING THE FAITHFUL TO PRAYER.

AT THE CHRISTMAS MASS.
ADESTE FIDELES...
THE BEAUTIFUL CHRISTMAS CAROLS SUNG BY THE CHILDREN'S CHOIR, REHEARSED IN SECRET WITH SISTER LAGRAVE, ENCHANTS THE CONGREGATION DURING MIDNIGHT MASS.
OH, THESE FAMILIAR CHRISTMAS CAROLS OF MY YOUTH !
ON APRIL 5, 1845, A MÉTIS GIRL, MARGUERITE CONNOLLY, JOINS THE SISTERS OF CHARITY AS A NOVICE.
MARGUERITE SPEAKS THE CREE LANGUAGE, WHICH PROVES USEFUL IN HER WORK WITH FIRST NATIONS PEOPLE.
PROVENCHER LACKS PRIESTS TO ASSIST HIM IN THE ESTABLISHMENT OF THE CHURCH AT RED RIVER. THE OBLATES OF MARY IMMACULATE, A RELIGIOUS MISSIONARY ORDER FROM FRANCE, AGREE TO HELP.
ON JUNE 24, 1845, FATHER AUBERT AND BROTHER TACHÉ LEAVE MONTRÉAL IN A BIRCHBARK CANOE HEADING TO RED RIVER.
HBC
THE BRIGADE IS ALSO CARRYING TWO GREY NUNS, SENT AS AIDES TO THEIR FARAWAY CONVENT.
TWO MONTHS LATER...
WELCOME TO RED RIVER, DEAR COLLEAGUES ! FINALLY, OBLATE MISSIONARIES, COMING TO HELP !
THANK YOU, YOUR GRACE.
I AM FATHER AUBERT.
AND YOUR YOUNG COMPANION?
LET ME INTRODUCE ALEXANDRE-ANTONIN TACHÉ.
A PRIEST?
NOT YET.
A DEACON, THEN?
A SUB-DEACON, YOUR GRACE.
SUB-DEACON !?
YET, I ASKED FOR PRIESTS !
BROTHER TACHÉ JUST TURNED 22 DURING OUR TRIP HERE.
HE'S ATTAINED THE CANONICAL AGE FOR ORDINATION. HE IS READY TO BE CONSECRATED, YOUR GRACE.
HUMPH ! I NEED MEN HERE... AND THEY SEND ME BOYS !
SOON, BISHOP PROVENCHER RECOGNIZES THE NOVICE'S COMPETENCE.

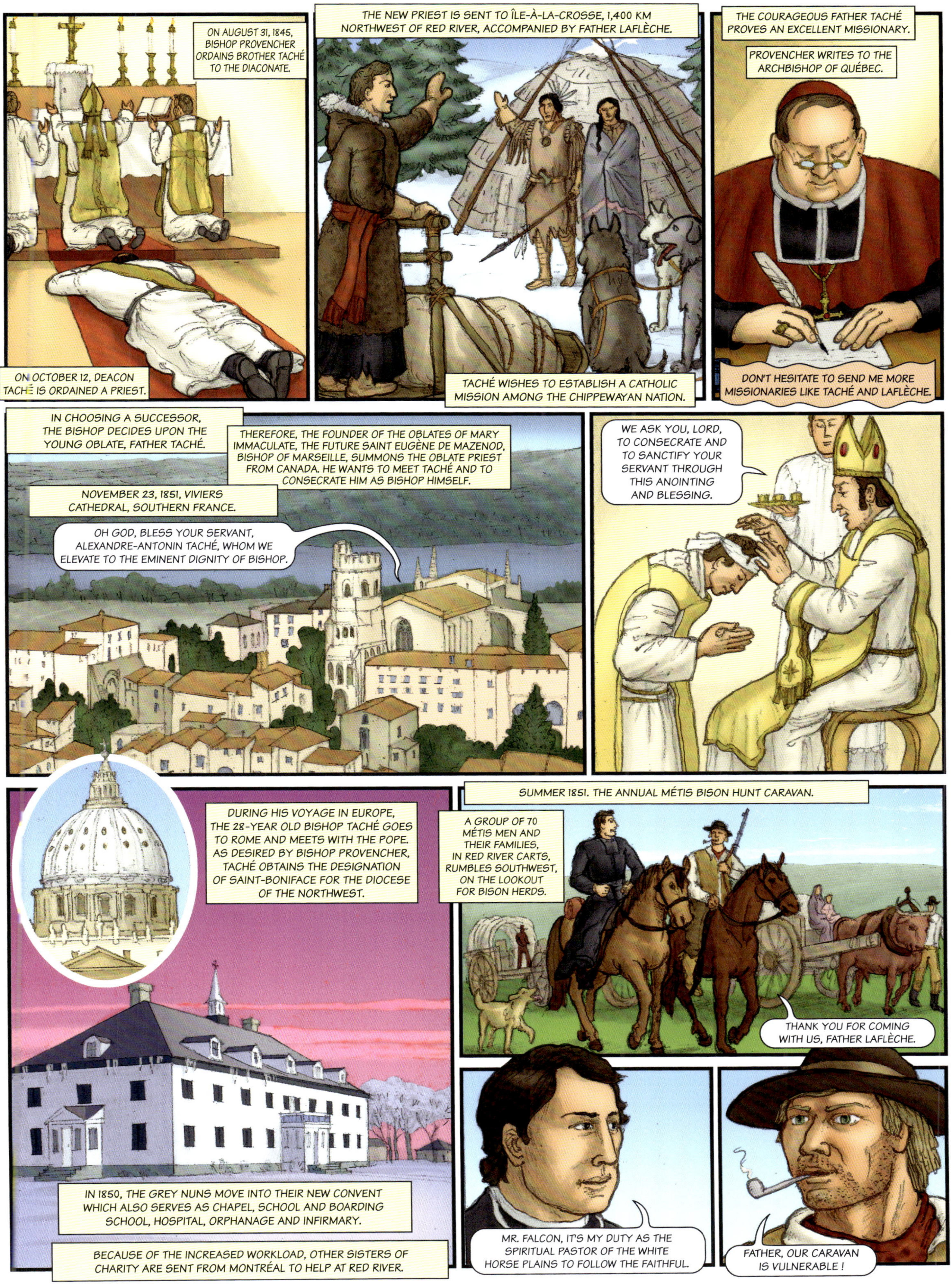

ON AUGUST 31, 1845, BISHOP PROVENCHER ORDAINS BROTHER TACHÉ TO THE DIACONATE.
ON OCTOBER 12, DEACON TACHÉ IS ORDAINED A PRIEST.
THE NEW PRIEST IS SENT TO ÎLE-À-LA-CROSSE, 1,400 KM NORTHWEST OF RED RIVER, ACCOMPANIED BY FATHER LAFLÈCHE.
TACHÉ WISHES TO ESTABLISH A CATHOLIC MISSION AMONG THE CHIPPEWAYAN NATION.
THE COURAGEOUS FATHER TACHÉ PROVES AN EXCELLENT MISSIONARY.
PROVENCHER WRITES TO THE ARCHBISHOP OF QUÉBEC.
DON'T HESITATE TO SEND ME MORE MISSIONARIES LIKE TACHÉ AND LAFLÈCHE.
IN CHOOSING A SUCCESSOR, THE BISHOP DECIDES UPON THE YOUNG OBLATE, FATHER TACHÉ.
THEREFORE, THE FOUNDER OF THE OBLATES OF MARY IMMACULATE, THE FUTURE SAINT EUGÈNE DE MAZENOD, BISHOP OF MARSEILLE, SUMMONS THE OBLATE PRIEST FROM CANADA. HE WANTS TO MEET TACHÉ AND TO CONSECRATE HIM AS BISHOP HIMSELF.
NOVEMBER 23, 1851, VIVIERS CATHEDRAL, SOUTHERN FRANCE.
OH GOD, BLESS YOUR SERVANT, ALEXANDRE-ANTONIN TACHÉ, WHOM WE ELEVATE TO THE EMINENT DIGNITY OF BISHOP.
WE ASK YOU, LORD, TO CONSECRATE AND TO SANCTIFY YOUR SERVANT THROUGH THIS ANOINTING AND BLESSING.
DURING HIS VOYAGE IN EUROPE, THE 28-YEAR OLD BISHOP TACHÉ GOES TO ROME AND MEETS WITH THE POPE. AS DESIRED BY BISHOP PROVENCHER, TACHÉ OBTAINS THE DESIGNATION OF SAINT-BONIFACE FOR THE DIOCESE OF THE NORTHWEST.
IN 1850, THE GREY NUNS MOVE INTO THEIR NEW CONVENT WHICH ALSO SERVES AS CHAPEL, SCHOOL AND BOARDING SCHOOL, HOSPITAL, ORPHANAGE AND INFIRMARY.
BECAUSE OF THE INCREASED WORKLOAD, OTHER SISTERS OF CHARITY ARE SENT FROM MONTRÉAL TO HELP AT RED RIVER.
SUMMER 1851. THE ANNUAL MÉTIS BISON HUNT CARAVAN.
A GROUP OF 70 MÉTIS MEN AND THEIR FAMILIES, IN RED RIVER CARTS, RUMBLES SOUTHWEST, ON THE LOOKOUT FOR BISON HERDS.
THANK YOU FOR COMING WITH US, FATHER LAFLÈCHE.
MR. FALCON, IT'S MY DUTY AS THE SPIRITUAL PASTOR OF THE WHITE HORSE PLAINS TO FOLLOW THE FAITHFUL.
FATHER, OUR CARAVAN IS VULNERABLE !

WE HAVE COME TO HUNT FOR OUR WINTER PROVISIONS, BUT WE HAVE A MAJOR PROBLEM...
WE'RE IN SIOUX TERRITORY !
WE HUNT HERE ON THE GRAND COTEAU, WHERE THE BISON ABOUND. BUT THE SIOUX SEE US AS ENEMY INTRUDERS.
SO, AT ANY MOMENT THEY COULD ATTACK US?
YES. THAT'S WHY I'VE SENT FIVE SCOUTS AHEAD OF THE CARAVAN, WHO 'LL WARN US OF ANY DANGER.
ALONG THE WAY, FATHER LAFLÈCHE MINISTERS TO HIS FLOCK. EVERY DAY HE CATECHIZES THE WOMEN AND CHILDREN, AND HE PRESIDES THE EVENING PRAYERS.
ON SUNDAYS, OBSERVED AS DAYS OF REST, HOLY MASS IS CELE-BRATED WITH THE ENTIRE CAMP.
A RED RIVER CART SERVES AS THE ALTAR, HARKING BACK TO THE ARK OF THE COVENANT ROAMING THROUGH THE DESERT.
THE SCOUTS MAKE A STARTLING DISCOVERY.
A HUGE CAMP OF SIOUX WARRIORS !
HOW MANY?
AT LEAST 2,000 !
AND THEY SEEM TO BE ON THE WARPATH !
THEY'RE GOING TO ATTACK OUR CARAVAN !
CRACK !
HUH?
SIOUX !
MÉTIS ! DO NOT MOVE ! YOU'RE SURROUNDED !

BUT TWO SCOUTS MANAGE TO ESCAPE.
THE SIOUX HAVE TAKEN THREE PRISONERS !
THEY'LL ATTACK !
CIRCLE THE WAGONS !
WOMEN AND CHILDREN UNDER COVER !
ALL THE ANIMALS INSIDE THE CIRCLE !
THE CARTS ARE POSITIONED TO FORM A CIRCULAR BARRICADE.
IN THE MIDDLE OF THE IMPROVISED FORT, THE WOMEN AND CHILDREN DIG TRENCHES AND TAKE COVER.
ALL THE MATERIAL IS PILED UP TO FORM PROTECTIVE WALLS
THERE THEY ARE !
TAKE YOUR POSITIONS EVERYONE !
A CAVALCADE OF SIOUX WARRIORS ENCIRCLES THE ENCAMPMENT.
THE MÉTIS HAVE DUG A TRENCH OUTSIDE THE CIRCLE OF WAGONS.
YIP ! YIP ! YIP !
BANG !
BANG !
POW !
POW !
FATHER LAFLÈCHE ENCOURAGES THE COMBATANTS.
THUD !
BE STRONG ! FIGHT BRAVELY !
GOD COMMANDS THAT YOU DEFEND YOUR WOMEN AND YOUR CHILDREN AND THAT YOU PROTECT THEM !
POW
DIE IF YOU MUST, BUT DIE WITH COURAGE !
WHILE THE WOMEN RELOAD THE MUSKETS, THE EXPERIENCED BISON HUNTERS SHOOT TO KILL.
THERE'S NO END TO THESE SIOUX WARRIORS !
BANG !
AND WE'RE RUNNING OUT OF AMMUNITION !
AAARGH !
DESPITE THEIR FAR SUPERIOR NUMBERS, THE SIOUX TAKE HEAVY LOSSES.
YOUNG MAN, YOU SURE CAN HANDLE THAT GUN !
YES, FATHER !
HOW OLD ARE YOU?
13 YEARS OLD.
YOU FIGHT LIKE A LION !
POW !
WHAT'S YOUR NAME?
GABRIEL DUMONT.

THE BATTLE STRETCHES ON FOR TWO DAYS. THE SIOUX HAVE LOST OVER 80 WARRIORS AND MANY MORE ARE WOUNDED.
C-CRRRAACK !
THERE IS A MANITOU WITH THE MÉTIS !
WE CANNOT WIN THIS BATTLE !
LET'S GET OUT OF HERE !
MÉTIS ! YOU ARE BRAVE WARRIORS ! NEVER AGAIN SHALL WE ATTACK YOU !
THE CARAVAN QUIETLY MAKES ITS WAY BACK TO RED RIVER.
WHAT ARE OUR LOSSES, JEAN-BAPTISTE?
NO LIVES LOST EXCEPT FOR POOR MALATERRE, OUR SCOUT, WHO WAS CAPTURED AND KILLED.
...AND A FEW WOUNDED.
THE WOMEN AND CHILDREN ARE SAFE AND SOUND?
YES, EVERYONE.
THANK GOD !
FATHER, YOUR PRAYERS AND YOUR ENCOURAGEMENT HELPED TO MAKE THIS MIRACLE POSSIBLE !
ON JUNE 27, 1852, BISHOP PROVENCHER WELCOMES HIS NEWLY APPOINTED COADJUTOR, BISHOP TACHÉ, JUST BACK FROM ROME.
BUT TACHÉ MUST LEAVE AGAIN IMMEDIATELY FOR THE FARAWAY MISSION OF ÎLE-À-LA-CROSSE.
PLEASE BLESS ME, YOUR GRACE.
IT'S UNCOMMON FOR A BISHOP TO BLESS ANOTHER, BUT I MAY SOON DIE AND NOT EVER SEE YOU AGAIN, SO I BLESS YOU NOW, WHILE AWAITING THE MOMENT I EMBRACE YOU IN HEAVEN.
ON JUNE 6, 1853, AT THE BISHOP'S PALACE IN ST. BONIFACE, PROVENCHER IS ON HIS DEATHBED.
SISTER LAGRAVE, I TOLD MY PRIESTS TO MAKE SURE THAT YOUR SISTERS NEVER LACK FOR ANYTHING
THANK YOU YOUR GRACE.
LET'S PRAY THE ROSARY.
YES, LET'S PRAY.
...HOLY MARY, MOTHER OF GOD, PRAY FOR US SINNERS, NOW AND...
...AND AT THE HOUR OF OUR DEATH...
THE CHURCH HAS JUST LOST A GREAT APOSTLE !
BUT BISHOP TACHÉ, WHO IS TO REPLACE PROVENCHER, IS STILL VERY FAR AWAY.

TACHÉ CONTINUES HIS MISSIONARY WORK AMONG THE CHIPPEWYANS FOR ANOTHER YEAR.
FINALLY, ON NOVEMBER 5, 1854, HE RETURNS FROM THE NORTH TO ASSUME HIS DUTIES AS THE NEW BISHOP OF ST. BONIFACE AT RED RIVER.
BISHOP TACHÉ PRIORITIZES FARAWAY MISSIONS AND EDUCATION FOR YOUTH. HE FOUNDS FOUR ELEMENTARY SCHOOLS AND THE ST. BONIFACE COLLEGE.
IN AUGUST, 1854, HE INVITES FOUR CHRISTIAN BROTHERS FROM MONTRÉAL TO COME TO THE COLONY AS EDUCATORS FOR THE BOYS.
IN 1858, LOUIS RIEL, AGED 14 YEARS, EXCELS IN HIS STUDIES AT ST. BONIFACE COLLEGE.
SISTER VALADE IS LEAVING FOR MONTRÉAL.
I'M SENDING THREE BRILLIANT YOUNG MEN TO SEMINARIES IN CANADA.
MAY THEY ACCOMPANY YOU ON YOUR JOURNEY?
YES, OF COURSE.
THANK YOU, SISTER.
TAKE GOOD CARE OF THEM.
THE YOUNG RIEL, IN PARTICULAR, IS A PROMISING YOUNG MAN. HE HAS POTENTIAL FOR PRIESTHOOD.
ON DECEMBER 14, 1860, PROVENCHER'S CATHEDRAL IS CONSUMED BY A TERRIBLE FIRE. ONLY THE TABERNACLE, A FEW OBJECTS AND THE STATUE MADE BY SISTER LAGRAVE ARE SAVED. ALL THE PARISH REGISTERS AND CORRESPONDENCE ARE DESTROYED.
THE FOLLOWING SPRING, IN 1861, ANOTHER HARDSHIP BEFALLS THE COLONY: THE RED RIVER FLOODS THE WHOLE AREA AND DESTROYS EVERYTHING.
TACHÉ UNDERTAKES A FUNDRAISER, AS PROVENCHER DID BEFORE HIM, TO REBUILD THE CATHEDRAL.
HE TRAVELS TO QUÉBEC AND TO FRANCE TO SOLICIT DONATIONS. THE CONSTRUCTION OF THE NEW CATHEDRAL COMMENCES IN 1862.

MEANWHILE, LOUIS RIEL STUDIES AT THE SAINT-SULPICE SEMINARY IN MONTRÉAL.
HERE TOO, HE IS OFTEN TOP OF CLASS IN MATHEMATICS, PHILOSOPHY, FRENCH AND ENGLISH LITERATURE, LATIN AND GREEK.
HE HAS A POET'S SOUL.
ON FEBRUARY 17, 1864, HE LEARNS OF THE DEATH OF HIS FATHER AT RED RIVER.
HE IS GRIEVING AND DISILLUSIONED. HE QUESTIONS THE MEANING OF LIFE.
RIEL LEAVES THE SEMINARY AND FINDS EMPLOYMENT AS A CLERK IN A LEGAL FIRM IN MONTREAL.
AND SOON...
MARIE-JULIE, I LOVE YOU.
MY FATHER WOULD NEVER ACCEPT OUR ENGAGEMENT.
BUT, WHY NOT?
BECAUSE YOU'RE MÉTIS, AND THEREFORE OF AN INFERIOR RACE, ACCORDING TO HIM.
HE'S SENDING ME FAR AWAY.
MARIE-JULIE, NOTHING COULD EVER...
LOUIS, WE'LL NEVER SEE EACH OTHER AGAIN !
DISCOURAGED, RIEL LEAVES MONTRÉAL.
AND AT RED RIVER...
YOUR GRACE, ANY NEWS FROM YOUR TALENTED PROTÉGÉ, LOUIS RIEL?
HE'S LEFT THE SEMINARY !
PARDON ME?
AND NO ONE SEEMS TO KNOW WHERE HE IS !
MY LORD !
RIEL MAKES HIS WAY BACK TO RED RIVER VIA THE UNITED STATES.
OVER THE NEXT TWO YEARS, HE WORKS AT SEVERAL JOBS.
DURING THIS PERIOD, IN 1867, CANADA ENTERS INTO CONFEDERATION.
QUÉBEC, ONTARIO, NEW BRUNSWICK AND NOVA SCOTIA JOIN TOGETHER TO FORM THE NEW DOMINION OF CANADA.
‹ ALL OF THIS TERRITORY IN AMERICA, NORTH OF THE UNITED STATES, COULD BE INTEGRATED INTO CONFEDERATION. ›
‹ OF COURSE ! OUR DOMINION WOULD THEN EXTEND FROM ONE OCEAN TO THE OTHER ! ›
THE FIRST PRIME MINISTER OF CANADA, JOHN ALEXANDER MACDONALD, AND HIS FRANCOPHONE LIEUTENANT, GEORGE-ÉTIENNE CARTIER, ARE AMBITIOUS.
‹ WELL, IN FACT, OUR NEGOTIATIONS ARE WRAPPING UP ! CANADA WILL SOON BE ABLE TO BUY AND ANNEX THIS TERRITORY FROM THE HUDSON'S BAY COMPANY ! ›
‹ GREAT ! GEORGE, LET'S SEND A TEAM OF SURVEYORS RIGHT AWAY TO PREPARE OUR ACQUISITION ! ›
HOWEVER, THE MOST IMPORTANT ELEMENT OF THE TRANSACTION HAS NOT BEEN CONSIDERED IN THEIR CAREFUL CALCULATIONS.
HAVE YOU HEARD? CANADA WANTS TO BUY OUR COLONY !
YES, WITHOUT CONSULTING US !
WE'RE BEING SOLD LIKE CATTLE !
AND THESE ARROGANT SURVEYORS ARE TRESPASSING ON OUR LANDS AS IF WE WEREN'T THERE !

IN JULY OF 1869, TACHÉ IS CALLED TO ROME.
I'M WORRIED ABOUT WHAT WILL HAPPEN AT THE COLONY WHILE YOU'RE AWAY, YOUR GRACE. THERE ARE SO MANY ENGLISH PROTESTANTS ARRIVING FROM ONTARIO, AND THEY SEEM TO HATE THE FRENCH !
WE'LL SOON BECOME A MINORITY !
IT WORRIES ME TOO, THE INCREASING PRESENCE OF THESE ORANGEMEN. THEY DO HARBOUR CONTEMPT FOR THE FRENCH CATHOLIC MÉTIS !
BUT TACHÉ MUST HEED THE CALL OF POPE PIUS IX.
HE CROSSES THE ATLANTIC TO ATTEND THE FIRST VATICAN COUNCIL IN ROME.
AT RED RIVER, RIEL AND THE MÉTIS TAKE MATTERS INTO THEIR OWN HANDS.
‹ CEASE YOUR SURVEYING AND LEAVE THIS LAND ! ›
‹ YOU'RE ON MÉTIS TERRITORY HERE ! YOU'LL GO NO FURTHER ! ›
‹ I'M FOLLOWING ORDERS ! ›
JANVIER, PUT YOUR FOOT ON THEIR CHAIN !
THUNK !
OH !
‹ YOU BETTER LEAVE, BEFORE YOU END UP IN THE RIVER ! ›
SPLOSH !
STILL, OTTAWA DESIGNATES A LIEUTENANT GOVERNOR AHEAD OF THE PURCHASE OF THE TERRITORIES OF THE NORTHWEST. WILLIAM MCDOUGALL MAKES HIS WAY TO RED RIVER VIA THE UNITED STATES.
THE MÉTIS LEARN THAT MCDOUGALL IS HIDING 350 RIFLES IN HIS LUGGAGE, TO QUELL ANY TYPE OF RESISTANCE WHEN HE ARRIVES AT RED RIVER.
ON OCTOBER 16, 1869, THE MÉTIS RALLY AROUND FATHER NOËL-JOSEPH RITCHOT, AT THE ST. NORBERT PRESBYTERY.
IT IS THEREFORE DECIDED THAT WE FORM, TODAY, THE MÉTIS NATIONAL COMMITTEE OF RED RIVER.
JOHN BRUCE IS ELECTED PRESIDENT AND LOUIS RIEL, SECRETARY. I MYSELF WILL ACT AS YOUR COUNSELLOR.
WE ARE AGREED THAT CANADA SHOWS US NO RESPECT AND THAT RESISTANCE IS NECESSARY.
FOR NOW, WE MUST PREVENT LIEUTENANT GOVERNOR MCDOUGALL FROM SETTING FOOT AT RED RIVER.
BEFORE HE SETTLES IN HERE, WE SHOULD HAVE OUR SAY CONCERNING THE TRANSFER OF OUR TERRITORY !

ON NOVEMBER 10, 1869, A MESSAGE, SIGNED BY LOUIS RIEL, IS SENT TO THE LIEUTENANT GOVERNOR, WARNING HIM TO STAY ON THE AMERICAN SIDE OF THE BORDER.
THE MÉTIS TAKE UP ARMS AND ERECT A BARRIER AT ST. NORBERT TO PREVENT ANY ENTRY INTO RED RIVER BY MCDOUGALL OR HIS EMISSARIES.
SOON...
‹ REMOVE THAT BLASTED FENCE ! ›
‹ YOU'LL GO NO FURTHER ! ›
‹ AND YOU'LL BE GOING BACK TO THE AMERICAN BORDER UNDER MILITARY ESCORT ! ›
MEANWHILE, RIEL AND 120 MÉTIS SEIZE FORT GARRY WITHOUT FIRING A SHOT. THEY THUS GAIN CONTROL OF THE REGION.
RIEL INVITES THE SURROUNDING VILLAGES TO SEND REPRESENTATIVES TO DISCUSS THE NEXT MEASURES TO BE TAKEN.
BUT NOT EVERYONE IS IN AGREEMENT...
A GROUP OF ARMED ORANGEMEN BARRICADE THEMSELVES IN A STORE IN WINNIPEG.
RIEL FEARS THAT HIS OPPONENTS ARE PREPARING AN ATTACK. ALONG WITH 300 MÉTIS, AND EQUIPPED WITH TWO CANNON, HE LAYS SIEGE TO THE FORTIFIED BUILDING.
48 ORANGEMEN SURRENDER AND ARE IMPRISONED.
ON DECEMBER 8, 1869, THE MÉTIS PROCLAIM THE ESTABLISHMENT OF A PROVISIONAL GOVERNMENT FOR THE NORTHWEST.
SOON, ORANGEMEN INSURGENTS ATTACK AN INNOCENT PASSERBY, NORBERT PARISIEN.
FALSELY ACCUSED OF ESPIONAGE, THE MÉTIS IS BEATEN MERCILESSLY BY THIS GROUP OF MEN.
THOMAS SCOTT FINISHES HIM OFF WITH BLOWS TO THE HEAD WITH A HATCHET.
FOLLOWING FURTHER MISDEEDS, SCOTT IS CAPTURED BY THE MÉTIS AND IS IMPRISONED,
HE IS BROUGHT BEFORE A MILITARY TRIBUNAL AND IS CONDEMNED TO DEATH.
MARCH 4, 1870 AT NOON...
P-P-POW !
UNHH !
MEANWHILE, IN ROME...
BISHOP TACHÉ, THE NEWS FROM RED RIVER IS SOMBER...
PRIME MINISTER MACDONALD ASKS YOU TO RETURN AS SOON AS POSSIBLE TO APPEASE THE SITUATION.
HMM...MY HOMELAND CALLS... I HAVE TO RETURN RIGHT AWAY !
BACK IN OTTAWA, WITH THE PRIME MINISTER...
‹ MR. MACDONALD, TO GAIN THE MÉTIS' TRUST, YOU MUST RECOGNIZE THEIR RIGHTS. ›
‹ OF COURSE ! LET THEM SEND A DELEGATION AND WE SHALL NEGOTIATE ! ›
‹ DO YOU PROMISE A GENERAL PARDON, AN AMNESTY, FOR ALL THE MEMBERS OF THE PROVISIONAL GOVERNMENT REGARDING THEIR ACTS OF RESISTANCE ? ›
‹ I PROMISE ! ›

BACK AT RED RIVER, TACHÉ VISITS RIEL, NOW PRESIDENT OF THE PROVISIONAL GOVERNMENT AT FORT GARRY.
WHAT NEWS FROM OTTAWA?
THE CANADIAN GOVERNMENT WISHES TO NEGOTIATE WITH YOUR PROVISIONAL GOVERNMENT THE INCLUSION OF THESE TERRITORIES IN THEIR CONFEDERATION.
VERY WELL, WE'LL SEND A DELEGATION TO OTTAWA TO PRESENT OUR LIST OF RIGHTS.
WE DO WANT TO JOIN THE CANADIAN CONFEDERATION, BUT AS A PROVINCE WITH ALL ITS PRIVILEGES !
INCLUDING THE RIGHT TO OUR CATHOLIC SCHOOLS !
WHAT ABOUT THE AMNESTY? WILL THE MEMBERS OF OUR GOVERNMENT BE GUARANTEED IMMUNITY?
YES, ABSOLUTELY...
TO MAINTAIN ORDER, THIS PROVISIONAL GOVERNMENT HAS HAD TO DEAL WITH SERIOUS BUSINESS. WE WANT TO BE SURE OF IMMUNITY IN CASE OF PROSECUTION !
WELL, THE RIGHT HON. JOHN A. MACDONALD HIMSELF HAS PROMISED ME AN AMNESTY.
IN WRITING?
NO, BUT I WAS ASSURED THAT IT'S NOW ONLY A QUESTION OF PROTOCOL AND THAT YOU MAY PROCEED WITHOUT FEAR.
A DELEGATION OF THREE REPRESENTATIVES FROM RED RIVER, LED BY FATHER RITCHOT, ARRIVES IN OTTAWA.
THE TENACIOUS FATHER RITCHOT SUCCEEDS IN HIS NEGOTIATIONS.
‹ THIS NEW PROVINCE SHALL BE CALLED MANITOBA. ›
‹ IN THE NATIVE TONGUE, IT MEANS "THE GOD WHO SPEAKS". ›
THE CANADIAN PARLIAMENT ADOPTS THE MANITOBA ACT ON MAY 12, 1870. ON JUNE 24, RIEL'S PROVISIONAL GOVERNMENT CONSENTS TO JOINING THE CANADIAN CONFEDERATION.
WITH THE ROYAL ASSENT ON JULY 15, 1870, THE NEW PROVINCE CAN ELECT DEPUTIES TO THE COMMONS AND BE REPRESENTED IN THE SENATE.
FATHER RITCHOT RETURNS TO RED RIVER.
THE FRENCH LANGUAGE IS NOW PROTECTED AND SO ARE CATHOLIC SCHOOLS !
AND THE AMNESTY?
NOTHING IN WRITING, I'M AFRAID.
WHAT? STILL NOTHING? I WAS PROMISED...
AT THIS VERY MOMENT, 1,200 SOLDIERS ARE ON THEIR WAY TO ENSURE THE TAKE-OVER OF MANITOBA ! WITHOUT A WRITTEN GUARANTEE, I'M GOING TO HAVE TO FLEE !
RIEL IS BLAMED FOR THE EXECUTION OF THOMAS SCOTT, AND MANY SOLDIERS WANT TO AVENGE HIS DEATH.
THE UNDISCIPLINED TROOPS TERRORIZE THE MÉTIS AT RED RIVER.
FROM NOW ON, LOUIS RIEL IS A HUNTED MAN, CONSTANTLY TRACKED BY BOUNTY HUNTERS.
TACHÉ RETURNS SEVERAL TIMES TO OTTAWA...
‹ MR. MACDONALD, YOU PROMISED ME A GENERAL PARDON FOR ALL MEMBERS OF THE PROVISIONAL GOVERNMENT. ›
‹ WILL YOU BE KEEPING YOUR PROMISE? ›
‹ WHAT PROMISE? SHOW ME A DOCUMENT ! ›
‹ LISTEN, CANADA IS COMPLICATED ! ›
‹ QUÉBEC VENERATES RIEL, WHEREAS ONTARIO DESPISES HIM. WHAT AM I TO DO? ›
‹ IT'S A JUGGLING ACT ! ›
DESPITE THE THREATS OF THE ORANGEMEN, RIEL RETURNS TO MANITOBA. THREE TIMES HE IS ELECTED TO THE CANADIAN PARLIAMENT.
BUT THREE TIMES HE IS DENIED HIS SEAT IN THE HOUSE OF COMMONS. FINALLY, HE IS EXPULSED FROM PARLIAMENT, AND BANISHED FROM CANADA FOR FIVE YEARS.

IN DECEMBER, 1875, LOUIS RIEL HAS A NERVOUS BREAKDOWN. HE IS SENT TO AN ASYLUM IN QUÉBEC.
BISHOP TACHÉ PAYS HIM A VISIT.
LOUIS, HOW ARE YOU?
THE LORD HAS SPOKEN! THE DAY APPROACHES... ROME SHALL FALL!
BISHOP BOURGET SHALL BE THE POPE OF THE NEW WORLD! AND YOU, BISHOP TACHÉ, WILL BE HIS SUCCESSOR!
HE'S AS MAD AS A HATTER!
TACHÉ RETURNS TO RED RIVER...
YOUR GRACE, THE MÉTIS ARE GRUMBLING. THEY SAY THAT YOU PROMISED AN AMNESTY IN THE NAME OF THE CANADIAN GOVERNMENT AND YET, THIS AMNESTY HAS NEVER COME ABOUT. MOREOVER, THE ORANGEMEN ARE HUNTING DOWN RIEL AND PERSECUTING THE MÉTIS!
IT HURTS ME DEEPLY THAT MY OWN PEOPLE BELIEVE ME TO BE COMPLICIT IN OTTAWA'S LIES.
ON SEPTEMBER 22, 1871, THE DIOCESE OF ST. ALBERT IS CREATED, NEAR EDMONTON.
VITAL-JUSTIN GRANDIN IS NAMED ITS FIRST BISHOP BY THE POPE. TACHÉ THUS BECOMES ARCHBISHOP OF ST. BONIFACE.
THE RED RIVER MÉTIS' WAY OF LIFE CHANGES DUE TO THE WAVES OF IMMIGRANTS FLOODING INTO THE NEW PROVINCE. THE GOVERNMENT DOESN'T KEEP ITS PROMISES. THE MÉTIS DISPERSE, SOME MOVING WEST WITH THE HOPE OF PRESERVING THEIR TRADITIONAL WAYS. MANY FAMILIES SETTLE ALONG THE NORTH SASKATCHEWAN RIVER VALLEY.
THEY FORM COMMUNITIES SUCH AS ST. LAURENT AND BATOCHE.
BUT SOON, SURVEYORS SHOW UP AGAIN, TRESPASSING AND MEASURING OUT SETTLED LAND, WITHOUT ANY REGARD FOR THE MÉTIS INHABITANTS.
THE MÉTIS FEAR THE LOSS OF THEIR PARCELS OF LAND, TO WHICH THEY HOLD NO OFFICIAL TITLE.
SUMMER, 1884.
GABRIEL DUMONT AND THREE MEN ARE DELEGATED TO GO AND FIND LOUIS RIEL IN MONTANA WHERE HE IS NOW A TEACHER AT THE ST. PIERRE MISSION. HE IS MARRIED AND THE FATHER OF TWO CHILDREN.
LOUIS, YOUR EXILE IS NOW OVER. COME BACK WITH US TO CANADA TO HELP YOUR PEOPLE CLAIM THEIR RIGHTS. OTTAWA IS IGNORING ALL OF OUR PETITIONS!
AND, IN JULY, 1884...
PEOPLE OF THE SASKATCHEWAN, LET'S START WITH A PETITION ADDRESSED TO THE FEDERAL GOVERNMENT.
BRAVO! YES! LET'S DO THAT!
RIEL IS INVITED TO MANY MEETINGS, HELD IN BOTH FRENCH AND ENGLISH. HE INSPIRES HOPE THROUGHOUT THE REGION.
IN ST. ALBERT, BISHOP GRANDIN IS WORRIED.
YOUR GRACE, THE POLICE ARE SPYING ON RIEL'S EVERY MOVE!
OTTAWA IS IGNORING THE PEOPLE HERE. THE POLICE NOW FEAR A GENERAL UPRISING OF THE MÉTIS AND NATIVE PEOPLES, WHO ARE FRUSTRATED!
AND RIEL COULD BE THE SPARK THAT CAUSES THE EXPLOSION! ARCHBISHOP TACHÉ CERTAINLY WARNED ME— RIEL IS UNSTABLE!
ON SEPTEMBER 5, 1884, GRANDIN MEETS RIEL AT THE CHURCH IN BATOCHE.
YOUR GRACE, YOUR CLERGY DOESN'T RESPECT THE MÉTIS, WHO HAVE LEGITIMATE DEMANDS.
I'M NOT AWARE OF YOUR DEMANDS.
BUT I CAN TELL YOU THAT I WILL NOT TOLERATE ANY CONSPIRACIES.
YOUR PRIESTS PREACH OBEDIENCE TO AUTHORITY, BUT SAY NOTHING ABOUT JUSTICE!

RIEL'S PETITION FINALLY GETS A RESPONSE ON MARCH 4, 1885.
WHAT DOES IT SAY?
THEY PROMISE A CENSUS AND A COMMISSION OF INQUIRY...
... BUT DON'T ADDRESS ANY OF OUR DEMANDS !
IT'S TIME THE MÉTIS SHOWED THEIR TEETH !
THE MÉTIS BECOME AWARE THAT THE MOUNTED POLICE ARE ON THEIR WAY TO CRUSH ANY SIGNS OF REBELLION. THEY IMMEDIATELY TAKE UP ARMS AND FORM A PROVISIONAL GOVERNMENT.
ARMS AND MUNITIONS ARE SEIZED IN THE SURROUNDING STORES.
FEDERAL AGENTS ARE TAKEN PRISONER.
TELEGRAPH LINES ARE CUT.
POLICE ARE CONFRONTED.
BATOCHE CHURCH IS REQUISITIONED AS A HEADQUARTERS.
BISHOP GRANDIN AND HIS CLERGY ATTEMPT TO CALM THINGS DOWN.
THOSE WHO BEAR ARMS SHALL BE DENIED THE SACRAMENTS...
...INCLUDING THEIR FAMILIES !
120 NORTHWEST MOUNTED POLICE ARRIVE NEAR DUCK LAKE.
BOOM !
POW !
POW !
BANG !
THEY CONFRONT AN ARMED FORCE OF 200 MÉTIS AND A BATTLE ERUPTS.
THE MÉTIS LOSE FOUR MEN. AS FOR THE POLICE FORCE, 12 DIE AND 11 ARE WOUNDED.
OTTAWA MOBILIZES AN EXPEDITIONARY FORCE..
5,000 SOLDIERS ARE SENT WEST TO QUELL THE REBELLION.
CHUGGA - CHUGGA - CHUGGA
SSSSSSSSSS
MEANWHILE, BACK AT BATOCHE...
WHY ARE WE BEING HELD PRISONER IN OUR OWN PRESBYTERY?
BECAUSE IT'S POSSIBLE YOU'RE SPIES, WORKING FOR OTTAWA !
YOU'RE DENYING US THE SACRAMENTS, SO NOW RIEL IS OUR SPIRITUAL LEADER.
THIS IS HERESY !
AN IMMENSE ARMY INEXORABLY LUMBERS ACROSS THE CANADIAN PLAINS, HEADING TOWARDS BATOCHE.
250 BRAVE MÉTIS COMBATANTS PREPARE CAMOUFLAGED RIFLE PITS, UNDER GABRIEL DUMONT'S COMMAND.
THE ARMY ARRIVES AT BATOCHE AND OPENS FIRE ON THE MÉTIS.
TA-TA-TA-TA-TA-TA-TA-TA-TOW !

FROM THEIR CONCEALED RIFLE PITS, THE EXPERIENCED BISON HUNTERS KEEP GENERAL MIDDLETON'S TROOPS AT A DISTANCE.
THE MÉTIS MILITARY COMMANDER, GABRIEL DUMONT, DIRECTS HIS FIGHTERS FROM ONE TRENCH TO ANOTHER TO COUNTER ANY ENEMY ADVANCE.
WITH COURAGE AND CUNNING, THIS MASTER TACTICIAN MANAGES TO CHECKMATE, DURING THREE DAYS OF FIGHTING, THE FAR SUPERIOR FORCE OF THE CANADIAN ARMY.
LOUIS RIEL, THE POLITICAL AND SPIRITUAL LEADER OF THE MÉTIS, WANDERS AMONG THE RIFLE PITS, URGING THE COMBATANTS TO BE BRAVE.
AFTER FOUR DAYS OF FIGHTING, THE CANADIAN FORCE FINALLY OVERWHELMS THE POORLY ARMED MÉTIS RESISTANCE.
LOUIS RIEL SURRENDERS TO GENERAL MIDDLETON. GABRIEL DUMONT ESCAPES TO THE UNITED STATES.
RIEL IS FOUND GUILTY OF HIGH TREASON IN A REGINA COURTHOUSE.
‹ ...AND THAT YOU WILL BE TAKEN TO THE PLACE APPOINTED FOR YOUR EXECUTION AND THERE BE HANGED BY THE NECK UNTIL YOU ARE DEAD. ›
‹ AND MAY GOD HAVE MERCY ON YOUR SOUL. ›
WHILE AWAITING HIS EXECUTION...
FATHER, I WANT TO RETURN INTO THE ARMS OF THE HOLY MOTHER CHURCH.
I RENOUNCE ALL FORMS OF HERESY !
VERY WELL, MY SON. LET US PRAY...
RIEL'S DEATH SENTENCE UNLEASHES A CONTROVERSY OF NATIONAL AND INTERNATIONAL PROPORTIONS.
BISHOP TACHÉ PLEADS FOR MERCY.
THIS IS UNJUST !
THEY WANT TO HANG A MADMAN !
REGINA, NOVEMBER 16, 1885
I FORGIVE ALL THOSE WHO HAVE OFFENDED ME, AND I ASK FORGIVENESS OF THOSE I HAVE OFFENDED.
DURING THE RED RIVER RESISTANCE THE CHURCH SUPPORTED RIEL, BUT SHUNNED HIM DURING THE NORTHWEST REBELLION. FINALLY, IN DEATH, THERE IS RECONCILIATION WITH THIS SON OF THE RED RIVER.
PIE JESU DOMINE, DONA EIS REQUIEM. AMEN.
LOUIS RIEL FINDS ETERNAL REPOSE IN HIS NATIVE SOIL, AT THE FOOT OF THE SAINT BONIFACE CATHEDRAL.
AFTER RIEL'S DEATH, THE DEFENCE OF RELIGIOUS AND LINGUISTIC RIGHTS FOR FRANCOPHONES IS MAINTAINED BY THE CHURCH.
BISHOP ALEXANDRE-ANTONIN TACHÉ IS THE SECOND BISHOP AND THE FIRST ARCHBISHOP OF ST. BONIFACE— THE MOTHER CHURCH OF WESTERN CANADA AND THE GREAT NORTH. HE OVERSEES THE DEVELOPMENT AND CONSOLIDATION OF HIS VAST DIOCESE. THE ARCHBISHOP ESTABLISHES 23 MISSIONS, 25 PARISHES, 7 APOSTOLIC VICARIATES AND TWO DIOCESES. HE SUPPORTS EDUCATION FOR YOUTH, FIRST NATIONS MISSIONS, CHARITABLE WORKS, AND FRENCH-CANADIAN IMMIGRATION TO MANITOBA. HE IS A PROLIFIC WRITER.
THIS GREAT APOSTLE RENDERS UP HIS SOUL ON JUNE 22, 1894, AFTER 44 YEARS SERVING AS BISHOP AND ARCHBISHOP.

EPILOGUE

BISHOP LOUIS-PHILIPPE-ADÉLARD LANGEVIN – 1895–1915

ARCHBISHOP LANGEVIN ORGANIZES AN ARCHAEOLOGICAL EXPEDITION TO LAKE OF THE WOODS IN 1902 AND DISCOVERS THE RUINS OF FORT ST. CHARLES AS WELL AS A CRYPT CONTAINING THE REMAINS OF JEAN-BAPTISTE LAVÉRENDRYE, FATHER J.-P. AULNEAU, S. J., AND 19 OTHER VOYAGEURS, ALL KILLED BY THE SIOUX IN 1736. THE CLERGYMAN DECIDES, ON THE SPOT, TO FOUND LA SOCIÉTÉ HISTORIQUE DE SAINT-BONIFACE. THE REMAINS ARE MOVED AND LATER INTERRED AT A MONUMENT IN ST. BONIFACE CATHEDRAL CEMETERY.

THE KNIGHTS OF COLUMBUS MOVEMENT IS FOUNDED IN THE DIOCESE IN 1906.

FROM 1905 TO 1908, BISHOP LANGEVIN BUILDS THE MAGNIFICENT ST. BONIFACE BASILICA-CATHEDRAL, WORTHY MONUMENT TO THE MOTHER-CHURCH OF WESTERN CANADA.

NEW PARISHES, MOSTLY RURAL AND FRENCH-CANADIAN, FLOURISH. THE CATHOLIC CHURCH DEVELOPS INFRASTRUCTURE THROUGH INSTITUTIONS AND BUILDINGS, OFTEN DESIGNED IN THE NEOCLASSICAL STYLE. THE CHURCHES, PRESBYTERIES, CONVENTS, SCHOOLS AND PARISH HALLS CONSTITUTE, IN MANY CASES, THE HEART AND CHARACTER OF THESE VILLAGES.

MANY RELIGIOUS CONGREGATIONS ARRIVE IN THE ST. BONIFACE DIOCESE. THEY ARE CONSECRATED MEN AND WOMEN WHO DEDICATE THEMSELVES TO EDUCATION, HEALTH CARE AND PASTORAL ACTIVITIES.

THE OBLATE FATHERS LAUNCH SEVERAL PUBLICATIONS SUCH AS LA LIBERTÉ IN FRENCH, AS WELL AS PUBLICATIONS IN GERMAN, POLISH AND UKRAINIAN. THE ARCHDIOCESE PUBLISHES LES CLOCHES DE SAINT-BONIFACE.

THERE'S AN INCREASING INFLUX OF IMMIGRANTS TO WESTERN CANADA. THE MÉTIS AND FRENCH-CANADIANS ARE HENCEFORTH A MINORITY IN MANITOBA AND WESTERN CANADA.

ARCHBISHOP ARTHUR BÉLIVEAU – 1915–1955

ARCHBISHOP BÉLIVEAU FALLS ILL IN 1931, AND IS REPLACED IN HIS DUTIES BY THREE SUCCESSIVE COADJUTORS.

THE COADJUTORS :
BISHOP ÉMILE YELLE – 1933 -1941
BISHOP GEORGES CABANA – 1941–1952
BISHOP MAURICE BAUDOUX – 1952–1955

IN 1916, THE GOVERNMENT OF MANITOBA ENACTS THE THORNTON LAW, ABOLISHING INSTRUCTION IN FRENCH. THE FRANCOPHONE COMMUNITY, IN COLLABORATION WITH THE CLERGY, REACTS BY CREATING A PARALLEL CLANDESTINE SCHOOL SYSTEM MAINTAINING FRENCH AS THE TEACHING LANGUAGE. THE SCHOOL SYSTEM IS NAMED L'ASSOCIATION D'ÉDUCATION DES CANADIENS-FRANÇAIS DU MANITOBA (AECFM).

THE ST. BONIFACE ARCHDIOCESE IS FRAGMENTED IN 1915, FOLLOWING THE FORMATION OF THE ARCHDIOCESE OF WINNIPEG. ARCHBISHOP BÉLIVEAU LEAVES FOR ROME TO NEGOTIATE AN ACCEPTABLE PARTITION OF THE TERRITORY.

THE RESIDENTIAL SCHOOLS SYSTEM, AN EDUCATIONAL STRATEGY EXTREMELY DETRIMENTAL TO FIRST NATIONS FAMILIES, DESIGNED TO ASSIMILATE THE YOUNGER GENERATION INTO A EUROCENTRIC CULTURE, IS ESTABLISHED BY THE FEDERAL GOVERNMENT, WHO ASSIGNS ITS IMPLEMENTATION TO MOSTLY CATHOLIC AND PROTESTANT INSTITUTIONS.

THE ST. BONIFACE CLERGY OF THIS ERA ARE PROMOTERS OF SOCIAL CHANGE THROUGH L'ACTION CATHOLIQUE AND THE MOUVEMENT COOPÉRATIF. THEY INITIATE THE CAISSES POPULAIRES MOVEMENT IN MANITOBA AND THE FRENCH RADIO STATION, CKSB.

IN 1946, LE GRAND SÉMINAIRE DE SAINT-BONIFACE IS FOUNDED.

DURING THIS PERIOD, THERE IS MUCH SUFFERING DUE TO THE GREAT DEPRESSION AND TWO WORLD WARS.

ARCHBISHOP MAURICE BAUDOUX – 1955–1974

ARCHBISHOP BAUDOUX AND HIS CLERGY ARE VERY SUPPORTIVE OF THE FRENCH-CANADIAN CULTURE IN THE WEST.

IN 1968, THE AECFM IS REPLACED BY THE SFM (SOCIÉTÉ FRANCO-MANITOBAINE), WHICH HAS A MANDATE TO DEFEND THE RIGHTS OF FRANCO-MANITOBANS.

LOBBYING FOR THE CONSTITUTIONAL RIGHT TO EDUCATION IN FRENCH BEGINS TO PRODUCE RESULTS.

THE FIRST FESTIVAL DU VOYAGEUR IS HELD IN 1970.

IN 1953, AS COADJUTOR, BISHOP BAUDOUX OFFICIALLY NAMES THE HOLY VIRGIN MARY OF THE IMMACULATE CONCEPTION THE PATRON SAINT OF THE ARCHDIOCESE OF ST. BONIFACE.

THE SEMINARY OF THE MOTHER CHURCH OF THE WEST TRAINS CLERGY FOR WESTERN CANADA AND ALSO FOR FOREIGN LANDS.

IN 1962, THE ARCHBISHOP PARTICIPATES IN THE SECOND VATICAN COUNCIL IN ROME, WITH THE YOUNG THEOLOGIAN PRIEST AND FUTURE ARCHBISHOP, ANTOINE HACAULT.

THE POST-VATICAN II TRANSITION IN THE DIOCESE IS INTENSE. THE LANGUAGE OF THE FAITHFUL REPLACES LATIN IN THE MASS. RITUAL AND DECOR ARE SIMPLIFIED AND THE PRIEST AT THE ALTAR NOW FACES THE ASSEMBLY.

CERTAIN PARISHES ARE TAKEN UP IN AN ICONOCLASTIC MOVEMENT. CHURCHES ARE STRIPPED OF THEIR STATUES, MURALS, PAINTINGS, ELABORATE DECOR AND TRADITIONAL ORNAMENTS.THE FRENCH-CANADIAN NEOCLASSICAL ARCHITECTURAL STYLE IS SET ASIDE.

THE CHARITABLE ORGANIZATION, DEVELOPMENT AND PEACE, IS FOUNDED IN 1967 BY THE CANADIAN CONFERENCE OF CATHOLIC BISHOPS. MANITOBA'S CHAPTER IS VERY ACTIVE.

THE SEMINARY OF THE ARCHDIOCESE OF ST. BONIFACE AND THE BOYS' COLLEGE RUN BY THE OBLATE FATHERS, LE JUNIORAT, BOTH CLOSE THEIR DOORS. THERE IS AN EXODUS OF PRIESTS, BROTHERS AND SISTERS FROM CONSECRATED RELIGIOUS LIFE.

IN 1968, THE IMPOSING CATHEDRAL-BASILICA OF ST. BONIFACE IS DESTROYED BY A GREAT FIRE. IN 1972, A NEW CATHEDRAL IS CONSECRATED, CONSTRUCTED WITHIN THE RUINS OF THE FORMER CATHEDRAL.

ARCHBISHOP ANTOINE HACAULT – 1974–2000

THROUGH THE RENEW PROGRAMME, SMALL PRAYER GROUPS ARE FORMED IN THE PARISHES.

THE NATHANAËL PROGRAMME OFFERS ADULT FAITH-BASED EDUCATION.

THE RENEWAL OF THE CHURCH, BEGUN AT VATICAN II COUNCIL, CONTINUES. PARISH PASTORAL COUNCILS, PROGRAMMES FOR YOUTH, AND FAMILY SERVICES ARE ESTABLISHED.

FORTY PARISHES SPONSOR REFUGEES FROM LAOS, VIETNAM AND CAMBODIA. THESE IMMIGRANTS FORM THEIR OWN CATHOLIC COMMUNITIES.

THE ARCHDIOCESE MUST DEAL WITH A GENERAL DECREASE IN THE NUMBER OF FAITHFUL ATTENDING SUNDAY MASS.

THE CONSTITUTIONAL RIGHTS OF FRANCO-MANITOBANS ARE PROGRESSIVELY RESTORED, DUE TO RULINGS IN THE COURTS OF LAW. THE YEAR 1994 MARKS THE ADVENT OF THE DIVISION SCOLAIRE FRANCO-MANITOBAINE.

THE PARISHES BEGIN TO EXPERIENCE THE EFFECTS OF A SHORTAGE OF PRIESTS. SOME SUNDAY SERVICES ARE PRESIDED BY LAY PERSONS, WITHOUT THE PRESENCE OF A PRIEST.

SOME MEMBERS OF THE CLERGY ARE SUBJECT TO ALLEGATIONS OF SEXUAL MISCONDUCT.

POPE JOHN PAUL II VISITS MANITOBA IN 1984.

RELIGIOUS COMMUNITIES' MEMBERS ARE AGING. THE LAITY BECOMES MORE ACTIVE IN THE LITURGY AND IN RELIGIOUS INSTITUTIONS.

ARCHBISHOP ÉMILIUS GOULET – 2001–2009

PARISHES THROUGHOUT THE DIOCESE PARTICIPATE IN A NEW MOVEMENT PROMOTING EVANGELISATION.

THE LAITY ASSUMES MANY OF THE ADMINISTRATIVE DUTIES IN THE PARISHES.

THE SPONSORSHIP OF REFUGEES FROM VARIOUS COUNTRIES CONTINUES.

THE CHURCH SENDS LAY PERSONS ON SHORT INTERNATIONAL MISSIONS.

DIOCESAN YOUTH DELEGATES ARE REGULARLY SENT TO PARTICIPATE AT WORLD YOUTH DAYS, HELD IN VARIOUS COUNTRIES.

A MARRIAGE AND FAMILY SERVICES SECTION IS CREATED AT THE ARCHDIOCESAN LEVEL.

IN 2003, THE SOCIÉTÉ FRANCO-MANITOBAINE FOUNDS L'ACCUEIL FRANCOPHONE, HELPING TO INTEGRATE IMMIGRANT FAMILIES AS THEY ARRIVE IN MANITOBA.

TO ADDRESS THE LACK OF CLERGY IN THE DIOCESE, PRIESTS FROM FOREIGN LANDS ARE SOLLICITED.

PRIORITIES INCLUDE THE FOSTERING OF VOCATIONS TO THE PRIESTHOOD AND THE TRAINING OF ASPIRING FOREIGN CANDIDATES.

ARCHBISHOP ALBERT LEGATT – JULY 3, 2009

ARCHBISHOP LEGATT IS ACTIVE IN EFFORTS TOWARDS RECONCILIATION WITH FIRST NATIONS AND THE MÉTIS.

ECUMENICAL ACTIVITIES AND CONSULTATIONS TAKE PLACE WITH OTHER CHRISTIAN COMMUNITIES AND MEMBERS OF OTHER RELIGIONS.

NEW PASTORAL INITIATIVES PROMOTE EVANGELISATION AND ADULT EDUCATION IN THE FAITH.

EFFORTS TO SUPPORT VOCATIONS TO THE PRIESTHOOD CONTINUE.

IN 2018, HALF OF ALL PRIESTS WORKING IN THE ARCHDIOCESE ARE FOREIGNERS.

SUPPORT IS ORCHESTRATED FOR REFUGEES FROM THE MIDDLE EAST AND AFRICA.

IN 1818, THE FAITHFUL OF THE MISSION AT RED RIVER, STRETCHING ALL THE WAY TO THE ROCKY MOUNTAINS, PRIMARILY MÉTIS AND FIRST NATIONS, ARE OF DIVERSE ORIGINS. IT IS MOSTLY FRANCOPHONES WHO WILL, DURING MORE THAN A CENTURY, STEER THE SHIP OF THE CATHOLIC CHURCH OF ST. BONIFACE. IN 2018, THE DIOCESE CONTINUES TO DIVERSIFY AS THE ENGLISH-SPEAKING FAITHFUL AND NEWCOMERS FROM VARIOUS COUNTRIES KEEP ARRIVING IN MANITOBA.

TRUE TO ITS ORIGINS AS THE RED RIVER MISSION, THE ST. BONIFACE ARCHDIOCESE, IN 2018, IS WELCOMING AND OPEN TO THE FUTURE.

THE 200TH ANNIVERSARY OF THE ARRIVAL OF FATHER PROVENCHER AT RED RIVER IS COMMEMORATED DURING THE YEAR 2018 WITH IMPORTANT EVENTS EMBRACED BY CATHOLICA 200, CELEBRATING THE RICH RELIGIOUS AND CULTURAL LEGACY OF THIS MOTHER-CHURCH OF 24 DIOCESES IN WESTERN CANADA AND THE GREAT NORTH.

TIMELINE

DATE	ARCHDIOCESE OF SAINT BONIFACE	MANITOBA, CANADA, THE WORLD AND THE CHURCH
15 000 B.C.		Arrival of first inhabitants in territory comprising modern-day Canada: Aboriginal peoples of Canada and their descendants.
1492		Christopher Columbus sets sail from Spain and makes landfall in America.
1534		Jacques Cartier departs Saint-Malo, France en route for America.
1641	Invited by the Ojibway, Jesuits travel to the eastern tip of Lake Superior.	
1654 -1656		Two *coureurs des bois*, Radisson and Desgroseillers, explore the West beyond Lake Superior, as far as Minnesota.
1694	Pierre Le Moyne d'Iberville, accompanied by Father Gabriel Marest, S.J., enter the mouth of the Nelson River in northern Manitoba.	
1731	La Vérendrye and his sons, Jean-Baptiste and François, accompanied by Charles-Michel Mésaiger, S.J., arrive at Rainy Lake. In 1732, they travel to Lake of the Woods with Cree and the Assiniboine guides.	
1734		La Vérendrye's men travel to The Forks.
1735	La Vérendrye and Father Jean-Pierre Aulneau, S.J., arrive at Fort Saint Charles in Lake of the Woods.	
1738		La Vérendrye and his sons reach the region now known as Saint Boniface. Further in the West, they establish Fort La Reine.
1763		Conquest and cession of New France to England. The Treaty of Paris brings an end to the Seven Years' War.
Circa 1770-80	The Métis play an important role in evangelization in Western Canada and in the North even before the arrival of the first missionaries. 	French-Canadian voyageurs settle in the West and, with their Aboriginal wives, give rise to a new people: the Métis of Western Canada. 
1783-84		Establishment of The North West Company.
1806		- The North West Company establishes Fort Gibraltar where the Red and Assiniboine rivers meet. - Marie-Anne Gaboury accompanies her husband, Jean-Baptiste Lagimodière, to the West; she is the first non-Aboriginal woman to settle there.
1811-1812	Founding of the Red River Colony by Lord Selkirk and Scottish and Irish settlers. Father Charles Bourke is chaplain of the first expedition.	
1812		- Peguis, the Saulteaux chief, helps the Selkirk settlers to establish themselves in the Red River Colony. - War of Independence of 1812 between the United States and Great Britain.
1816		The Battle of Seven Oaks.
1818	- Following the Métis petition, at the request of Lagimodière and finally under pressure by Lord Selkirk, Mgr Plessis, the bishop of the British colonies of North America, agrees to open a mission in the Red River Colony. - Arrival of Father Joseph-Norbert Provencher, Father Sévère Dumoulin and seminarian Guillaume Edge after a long journey by canoe (May 19 to July 16). Permanent establishment of the Catholic Church in Western Canada. - Inauguration of the first chapel under the patronage of Saint Boniface, November 1st.	Definition of the border between the United States and Canada at the 49th parallel, forcing the Métis of Pembina to come settle in Canada.
1819-25	Construction of the 2nd church of Saint Boniface.	
1820-22	- Arrival of Father Destroismaisons and Joseph Sauvé, a seminarian who replaced Edge. - Father Joseph Norbert Provencher is named bishop of Juliopolis in 1820. He accepts the role of auxiliary bishop of Quebec and vicar general of Quebec in 1821. He is consecrated as bishop on May 12, 1822. ►	1821 - Merger of the two fur-trading companies: North West and Hudson's Bay. 

DATE	ARCHDIOCESE OF SAINT BONIFACE	MANITOBA, CANADA, THE WORLD AND THE CHURCH
1822	Arrival of seminarian Jean Harper who replaced Sauvé.	Creation of the Council of Assiniboia.
1824	First sacerdotal ordination in the Red River Colony: Father Jean Harper.	
1829	A Catholic school for girls is opened in Saint Boniface by Angélique and Marguerite Nolin.	
1831	Father Georges-Antoine Belcourt arrives at the Red River Colony.	
1837		Upper Canada and Lower Canada Rebellions, 1837-38.
1839	Benediction and opening of the stone church in Saint Boniface (3rd church), of which construction had begun in 1832. It would become the 1st cathedral in 1847. ►	
1840		The Act of Union unites the two colonies of Upper Canada and Lower Canada under one government.
1844	The Red River district is separated from the Diocese of Quebec and is established as the apostolic vicariate of Hudson Bay and James Bay with Mgr Provencher as its titular bishop.	
1844	The Grey Nuns of Montreal arrive in Saint Boniface, Manitoba: Marie-Louise Valade, Eulalie Lagrave, Gertrude Coutlée and Hedwidge Lafrance. ►	
1845	The first Oblates arrive in the Red River Colony: Father Pierre Aubert and Brother Alexandre-Antonin Taché. ►	
1846	Erection of Diocese of Vancouver Island, with bishop residing in Victoria.	
1847	The apostolic vicariate of Hudson Bay and James Bay is elevated to the rank of diocese, from then on called the Diocese of the Northwest and attached to the ecclesiastic province of Quebec. Provencher is bishop of the Diocese of the Northwest; the church in Saint Boniface becomes the 1st cathedral of the diocese.	
1850	Father Alexandre-Antonin Taché, O.M.I., appointed Bishop of Arath and coadjutor to Mgr Provencher, with the right of succession. He is consecrated as bishop in 1851.	
1850	The name of the Diocese of the Northwest changes to the Diocese of Saint Boniface.	
1853	Mgr Joseph-Norbert Provencher dies at the age of 66.	

1818 to 1853 – Era of Mgr Provencher. Period of numerous and intense visits by missionaries among Aboriginal people in the apostolic vicariate of Hudson Bay and James Bay; period of learning Aboriginal languages and beginning of evangelization. Establishment of 9 central missions serving other locations. Foundation of one parish: Saint Boniface. Erection of an apostolic vicariate. Erection of 2 diocese.

1854	**Mgr Taché becomes bishop of Saint Boniface on November 5th.** ► -Father Vital-Justin Grandin, O.M.I., arrives in Saint Boniface. -The Christian Brothers arrive. They agree to lead the boys' school and *Collège de Saint-Boniface*.	
1857	Vital-Justin Grandin, O.M.I., is appointed titular bishop of Satala and coadjutor to Mgr Alexandre-Antonin Taché, O.M.I. He is consecrated on November 30, 1859.	
1859		The first steamboat, The Ansom Anthrup, arrives in Manitoba at The Forks and Saint Boniface.

DATE	ARCHDIOCESE OF SAINT BONIFACE	MANITOBA, CANADA, THE WORLD AND THE CHURCH
1860	- The Oblates assume leadership of *Collège de Saint-Boniface* after the departure of the Christian Brothers. Father Jean-Marie LeFloc'h is named its director. - Benediction by Mgr Taché of a school led by the Grey Nuns for the Métis of Saint Vital, which later became the parish of Saint Vital. - Fire destroys the cathedral built by Mgr Joseph-Norbert Provencher.	
1861		- Flooding of the Red River Colony. - Civil war in the United States (1860-1865).
1863	Reconstruction of the cathedral and bishop's palace (4th church, 2nd cathedral). 	
1867		Canadian Confederation: Quebec, Ontario, Nova Scotia and New Brunswick.
1869	Pius IX opens the First Vatican Council. Mgr Taché is in attendance but he is called back to Canada at the request of the government due to events transpiring at the Red River Colony.	- Uprising at the Red River Colony. - Louis Riel forms provisional government. 
1870		The provisional government, presided by Louis Riel, adopts a code of law, from which several articles are later integrated into the Manitoba Act. Manitoba becomes the fifth province to join the Confederation.
1871	- Saint Boniface is raised to the rank of metropolitan see, with the foundation of the Diocese of Saint Albert (Edmonton after 1912), and Mgr Taché becomes archbishop of the ecclesiastic province of Saint Boniface. - Father Théophile Lavoie, O.M.I., obtains legal incorporation of *Collège de Saint-Boniface*. - The Grey Nuns establish the Hospital of Saint Boniface, the first hospital in Western Canada. 	 - Opening of the first session of the Manitoban Legislature. - Adoption of the first Education Act: the law creates a department of education with two sections, Catholic and Protestant. - The first issue of the weekly *Le Métis* is published.
1873		- Winnipeg is incorporated as a city. - On March 12, the first electric lightbulb is turned on in Winnipeg at the hotel Davis House on Main Street.
1874	The Sisters of the Holy Names of Jesus and Mary arrive in Manitoba: Exilia Nault, Georginie Duhamel and Clémence Cadieux.   	

DATE	ARCHDIOCESE OF SAINT BONIFACE	MANITOBA, CANADA, THE WORLD AND THE CHURCH
1877	Incorporation of *Collège de Saint-Boniface* with St. John's College and Manitoba College to establish the University of Manitoba.	The first locomotive on the Prairies, the Countess of Dufferin, arrives at The Forks and Saint Boniface on a barge pushed by the Selkirk steamboat.
1880	Arrival of the Marianist Brothers in Manitoba.	- Arrival of the first Canadian Pacific train in Winnipeg. - The telephone appears in Winnipeg in 1880-81, but most significantly in 1908, with the arrival of the company Manitoba Government Telephones.
1883	Arrival of five religious from the Faithful Companions of Jesus – school in Brandon.	- Creation of the village of Saint Boniface. - The CPR crosses the Blackfoot Reserve. Father Albert Lacombe, O.M.I., is an important negotiator between Chief Crowfoot and the government to make this possible. 
1885	- The Jesuits arrive in Manitoba and assume direction of *Collège de Saint-Boniface*.  - *The Northwest Review*, the first Catholic newspaper in the West, is published for the first time.	- The Rebellion of 1885 and the Métis uprising.  - Louis Riel is hung in Regina, Northwest Territories.
1889	Provincial Council of Saint Boniface (July 16 to 24), convened to evaluate the development of the Catholic Church in the West.	
1890	Edouard Conningham becomes the first Aboriginal person to be ordained by the Catholic Church on March 19, 1890, by Mgr Vital Grandin.	- Abolition of the Catholic and Protestant public education system in Manitoba. Suppression of the French language as the official language in the courts and Legislative Assembly of Manitoba. - Francophones in Winnipeg establish the Société Saint-Jean-Baptiste to defend their language and their faith.
1891	The Regular Canons of the Immaculate Conception arrive in Notre Dame de Lourdes.	
1892	The Trappists establish their monastery in Saint Norbert.	Inauguration of the first streetcar in Winnipeg. 
1894	Death of Mgr Alexandre-Antonin Taché, O.M.I.	

1853 to 1894 – Era of Mgr Alexandre-Antonin Taché. Period of development and consolidation of archdiocese. Evangelization in the North West and Prairies. Establishment of 23 central missions serving other locations. Founding of 25 parishes and canonical erection of 18 parishes. Erection of 7 apostolic vicariates. Erection of 2 diocese.

DATE	ARCHDIOCESE OF SAINT BONIFACE	MANITOBA, CANADA, THE WORLD AND THE CHURCH
1895	**Mgr Adélard Langevin, O.M.I., becomes 3rd bishop, 2nd archbishop of Saint Boniface.** 	
1895	The Canonesses Regular of the Five Wounds of the Saviour (Sisters of the Saviour) arrive in Notre Dame de Lourdes in Manitoba.	
1896		- Wilfrid Laurier becomes prime minister of Canada. From 1896-1914, Laurier makes a concerted effort to attract European and American immigrants to the Canadian Prairies. - Adoption of the Laurier-Greenway Compromise.
1897	Arrival of the Franciscaines Missionnaires de Marie.	
1898	- Arrival of the Sisters of Misericorde in Manitoba. They assume management of Misericordia Hospital in Winnipeg. - Arrival of the Redemptorists – parish in Brandon. - Arrival of the Sisters of Our Lady of the Missions in Grande Clairière.	
1899	Founding of the parish of St. Nicholas (Ruthenian) in Winnipeg.	- Opening of a bilingual Normal School. Classes are held at the boarding school of the Sisters of the Holy Names. - The Marianist Brothers assume leadership of *École Provencher*.
1901	Arrival of the Sisters of Saint Joseph of Saint-Hyacinthe.	
1902	First publication of *Les Cloches de Saint-Boniface*.	Founding of the *Société historique de Saint-Boniface* by Mgr Adélard Langevin.
1903	- Arrival of the Basilian Fathers in Winnipeg upon invitation by Mgr Langevin, for the Ukrainian parish of St. Nicholas. - Arrival of two Fathers of Chavagnes: Fathers Loriau and Thibault; they settle in Cartier (Saint Adolphe). - Ordination of Louis-de-Gonzague Bélanger, 1st priest born in Manitoba, April 12, 1879. - The Sisters of Misericorde open a home for abandoned children (Ritchot Orphanage).	
1904	- Arrival of the Clerics of Saint Viator in Makinak, Manitoba. - Arrival of the Sisters of the Cross in Manitoba. - Canonical erection of the novitiate for a Manitoban religious community: Congregation of The Missionary Oblates of the Sacred Heart and of Mary Immaculate. ►	
1905	Founding of the *Juniorat de la Sainte-Famille*.	Creation of Saskatchewan and Alberta.
1906	Benediction of the 5th church and 3rd cathedral by Mgr Adélard Langevin. 	Founding of the Knights of Columbus, Winnipeg chapter, followed by the Brandon chapter in 1909.
1907		Founding of the German-language newspaper *Die West Canada* by the Oblates.

DATE	ARCHDIOCESE OF SAINT BONIFACE	MANITOBA, CANADA, THE WORLD AND THE CHURCH
1908		- Founding of the Polish-language newspaper *Gazeta Katolicka* by the Oblates. - The village of Saint Boniface becomes the city of Saint Boniface, the largest bilingual city in Western Canada.
1909	- Opening of the children's garden under the name of *Jardin Langevin*, led by The Missionary Oblates of the Sacred Heart and of Mary Immaculate. - Establishment of the *Petit Séminaire*.	Founding of the newspaper *Canadian Ruthenian* by the Oblates.
1911	- Canonical erection of St. Peter's Abbey. - Fire at the *Juniorat*, former site of the *École industrielle de Saint-Boniface*. - Construction begins on the *Petit Séminaire de Saint-Boniface*, which would become *Collège de Saint-Boniface* after the fire of 1922.	
1912	- Arrival of 12 Carmelite religious in Manitoba. - Election of Mgr Nykyta Budka, first exarch of Ruthenian Catholics. - Arrival of the Little Sisters of the Holy Family. - Arrival of the Sisters of the Order of St. Benedict in Manitoba.	
1913	- Consecration of Arthur Béliveau who is named bishop and auxiliary to Mgr. Adélard Langevin, O.M.I. - Arrival of the Marist Brothers in Sainte Anne des Chênes. - The Sisters of the Holy Names of Jesus and Mary open their new boarding school on De la Cathédrale Avenue.	Mgr Adélard Langevin establishes *La Liberté*, a politically independent Catholic French weekly. Until 1941, the newspaper is run by laypeople, including Donatien Frémont and Hector Hé-roux, brother of the founder of *Le Devoir*. The O.M.I. subsequently assume its management.
1914	Arrival of the Ursuline Sisters of Tildonk in Bruxelles, Manitoba.	Election of Pope Benedict XV.
1914-18		World War One.
1915	Mgr Louis-Philippe Adélard Langevin dies on June 15.	

1895 to 1915 – Era of Mgr Adélard Langevin. Period of the opening of Western Canada to large waves of immigration. The following developments are undertaken in response to changing needs: Founding of 14 central missions. Founding of 64 parishes and canonical erection of 37 parishes. Erection of 2 apostolic vicariates. Erection of 5 diocese and 3 archdiocese. In 1909, there were approximately 250 missions served by parishes.

1916	- Major changes occur following the death of Mgr Langevin: the Archdiocese of Saint Boniface is fractured. Mgr Béliveau travels to Rome with a delegation to ensure the continued viability of the Archdiocese of Saint Boniface. - Creation of the Archdiocese of Winnipeg: Mgr Alfred Arthur Sinnott is its first archbishop. **- Mgr Arthur Béliveau becomes 4th bishop and 3rd archbishop of Saint Boniface.**  - The diocese of Regina, erected on March 4, 1910, becomes an archdiocese in 1916 with Mgr Olivier Elzéar Mathieu as archbishop.	- The Thornton Act eliminates bilingual schools and abolishes education in French. The act also makes primary education mandatory for children in Manitoba. - Founding of the *Association d'éducation des Canadiens français du Manitoba* (AECFM), a quasi-parallel department of education with the mandate to improve education in French for Francophones of Manitoba. - Creation of the *Association des commissaires d'école de langue française du Manitoba*.

DATE	ARCHDIOCESE OF SAINT BONIFACE	MANITOBA, CANADA, THE WORLD AND THE CHURCH
1916-19		Suffragette movement. Women obtain the right to vote in Manitoba in 1916, and, by the mid-1920s, Canadian women in other provinces obtain the right to vote, with the exception of Quebec.
1918	- Arrival of the Sisters Adorers of the Precious Blood in Saint Boniface. - St. Mary's Church in Winnipeg, which belonged to the O.M.I., was given to the new archbishop of Winnipeg by Rome and became a Cathedral.	Opening of *Collège de Gravelbourg*, Saskatchewan.
1919		Winnipeg General Strike organized by the working class. 
1921	Canonical erection of St. Peter's as a territorial abbey.	
1922	Fire at *Collège de Saint-Boniface* – 10 fatalities (1 teacher and 9 students). 	Commercial radio introduced in Canada.
1923		- Fire at *Académie Provencher*. - First annual French competition hosted by the AECFM.
1924	- Arrival of the Missionaries of Our Lady of La Salette in Beausejour, Manitoba. - The monastery Notre-Dame-des-Prairies is erected as a priory.	
1925	Mgr Béliveau establishes the congregation Les *Petites Missionnaires de Saint-Joseph* of Otterburne. 	Founding of *Cercle Molière*, the oldest continually operating theatre company in Canada.
1926	Founding of *Scolasticat de Lebret*.	
1928	- Arrival of the Capuchin Fathers in Manitoba. They took leadership of the Sacre Cœur parish (Belgium). - Departure of the Carmelites.	
1929		- Start of the international economic crisis. - Founding of the *Cercle ouvrier Saint-Joseph.*
1931		The Statute of Westminster: Canada obtains its official status as an independent nation.
1932	The diocesan conference of the *Action Catholique de la Jeunesse Canadienne-française* unites 21 groups.	
1933	Consecration of Mgr Émile Yelle, P.S.S., archbishop and coadjutor of Saint Boniface. 	
1936	*Académie Saint-Joseph*, run by the Sisters of the Holy Names of Jesus and Mary, becomes affiliated with the University of Manitoba as the women's section of *Collège de Saint-Boniface*, under the name *Collège Saint-Joseph*.	

DATE	ARCHDIOCESE OF SAINT BONIFACE	MANITOBA, CANADA, THE WORLD AND THE CHURCH
1937	- Opening of a hospital at Berens River. - Father Adélard Couture is named director of *Action catholique diocésaine*. He acted as a propagandist for the cooperative movement for more than 20 years.	*La Caisse populaire de Saint-Malo* is the first legally registered credit union in Manitoba.
1938		Father Gontran Laviolette, O.M.I., establishes *The Indian Missionary Record*, serving Aboriginal clientele until 1987.
1939	First diocesan synod.	Start of World War Two.
1940		Canadian Publishers Limited, owned by the Oblates, acquires *Le Patriote*. The first issue of *La Liberté et Le Patriote* appears on April 23rd.
1941	- Mgr Georges Cabana is consecrated coadjutor to Mgr Béliveau. 	
1944	The Oblates agree to lead the spiritual retreats in Saint Boniface.	
1945		The federal government creates the first universal family benefits for children under 16 years of age.
1946	Official opening of the *Grand Séminaire de Saint-Boniface*, placed under the direction of the Father Oblates. In 1948, the direction of the *Grand Séminaire* was handed over to secular priests.	 - Creation of CKSB, first Francophone radio station outside of Quebec, created by donations from Francophones in Manitoba. - Creation of the *Conseil de la coopération in Manitoba*.
1947	Death of Mgr Émile Yelle, P.S.S.	- Creation of a folk dance troupe in Saint Boniface: *Les Gais Manitobains*. - Opening of Notre Dame Pool, built and managed by the Catholic parish of Saint Boniface.
1948	- Consecration of Mgr Maurice Baudoux, bishop of Saint-Paul, Alberta. - Official opening of the *Grand Séminaire de Saint-Boniface*. - Arrival of the White Fathers, Missionaries of Africa.	
1949	Missionary congress held in Saint Boniface on the topic of missionary education in residential schools.	
1950	Opening of the novitiate of the Oblates in Saint Norbert.	
1951	Second diocesan synod.	
1952		*Radio Canada* television hits the airwaves in Montreal.
1953	- Mgr Maurice Baudoux becomes archbishop-coadjutor of Saint Boniface.  - Official decree proclaims the Blessed Virgin Mary, under the title of the Immaculate Conception, patron of the diocese and ecclesiastic province of Saint Boniface.	

1954	Father Oscar Boily, S.J., named rector of *Collège de Saint-Boniface*. He is the first Manitoban-born rector.	
1955	Mgr Arthur Béliveau dies on September 14th.	

1915 to 1955 – Era of Mgr Arthur Béliveau. Time of sweeping changes but also continued growth. From 1931 until his death, Mgr Béliveau remained titular bishop but due to illness was unable to perform his duties. From 1933 to 1955, three archbishop-coadjutors took turns at the helm of the archdiocese. Founding of 10 missions. Founding of 23 parishes and canonical erection of 28 parishes. Erection of 2 diocese and one archdiocese. In 1950, there were approximately 89 missions served by parishes

1955	**Mgr Maurice Baudoux becomes the 5th bishop and 4th archbishop of Saint Boniface.**	The provincial government authorizes the teaching of French from 4th to 6th grade.
1956		The Hungarian Revolution – a large number of Hungarians seek refuge in Canada after the revolution.
1958		Pope John XXIII inaugurates his pontificate.
1959		A royal commission examining education recommends that French be allowed to be taught beginning in Grade 1.
1960	- Official opening of the Villa Maria retreat centre in Saint Norbert. - Arrival of a lay association, the *Auxiliaires Rurales Catholiques*, now known as *Groupe Monde et Espérance*.	- Inauguration of CBWFT, *Société Radio Canada's* French television channel. - Aboriginal people obtain the right to vote in federal elections.
1962	Mgr Baudoux participates in the Second Vatican Council. Father Antoine Hacault accompanies him under the title of theologian. 	Start of the Second Ecumenical Council of the Vatican by John XXIII. 
1963		Agreement between the Grey Nuns and municipal authorities that their convent, which was built in 1846, will house the Saint Boniface Museum.
1964	Father Antoine Hacault is named auxiliary bishop to Mgr Maurice Baudoux.  	

DATE	ARCHDIOCESE OF SAINT BONIFACE	MANITOBA, CANADA, THE WORLD AND THE CHURCH
1966		Official opening of the *Centre de Loisirs Saint-Louis.*
1967	- Founding of Development and Peace. - Jesuits cede administration *of Collège de Saint-Boniface* to the diocese of Saint Boniface. - Closing of the Oblate *Scolasticat* in Saint Norbert. - Closing of high schools *Académie Saint-Joseph*, led by the Sisters of the Holy Names of Jesus and Mary, for girls, and, *École Provencher*, led by the Marianist Brothers, for boys. - Opening of a coed bilingual secondary school: *Institut collégial Louis Riel Collegiate.*	- Adoption of Bill 59 – Right to teach in French in Manitoban schools up to 50% of time. - Founding of *100 Nons* at *Collège de Saint-Boniface.* - Centennial of Canada. - Expo 67: the Universal Exposition in Montreal.
1968	- Closing of the *Grand Séminaire de Saint-Boniface.* - Closing of the Oblate *Juniorat de la Sainte-Famille.* - Fire at the Saint Boniface Cathedral on July 22nd. 	The *Société franco-manitobaine* (SFM) is officially constituted.
1969	- Secularization of *Collège de Saint-Boniface*: new board of directors composed of 20 members, majority of whom are laypeople.	- Adoption of a federal law on official languages in Canada: right to receive services from the federal government in French or English. - Neil Armstrong becomes the first man to walk on the moon on July 21, 1969.
1970	- Arrival of the Sisters of the Holy Cross, C.S.C.	- First *Festival du Voyageur.*  - Adoption of Bill 113: French reclaims the place it held prior to 1916, as a language of instruction on equal footing with English in the public schools of Manitoba.
1972	- Benediction of the 6th church and 4th cathedral in Saint Boniface. - Mgr Antoine Hacault is appointed archbishop-coadjutor.	Year one of Unicity – The forced merger of 12 rural and urban municipalities in the Winnipeg metropolitan area. Saint Boniface ceases to exist as an autonomous city.
1973	Opening of *L'Arche Winnipeg.*	- Creation of the *Fondation Radio Saint-Boniface.* - Founding of the *Conseil jeunesse provincial* (CJP). - Invention of the mobile phone.

1955 to 1974 – Era of Mgr Maurice Baudoux, Archbishop of Saint Boniface. Period in which the Mother Church of the West, under the leadership of Mgr Baudoux, oversaw the training of clergy for the West, for elsewhere in Canada, as well as for South America. Period of creativity for supporting the development of French culture in the West and opening up to the world. Period of transition: priests laicize and religious leave their communities, decrease in vocations devoted to religious life; closing of institutions run by religious communities and secularization of some of these institutions. Founding of 5 missions. Founding of 6 parishes and canonical erection of 2 parishes. In 1964, there were approximately 105 missions served by parishes.

DATE	ARCHDIOCESE OF SAINT BONIFACE	MANITOBA, CANADA, THE WORLD AND THE CHURCH
1974	**Mgr Antoine Hacault takes over from Mgr Maurice Baudoux and becomes the 6th bishop and 5th archbishop of Saint Boniface.** 	
1975		Opening of *Collège communautaire de Saint-Boniface*.
1976	The Cistercian Fathers (*Notre-Dame-des-Prairies*) move from Saint Norbert to Holland, Manitoba.	First personal computer appears on the market.
1978	*Ad limina* visit to Rome – Mgr Hacault presents his quinquennial report and the pastoral priorities of his diocese: improvement of theological training for priests, training of laypeople, apostolate for youth.	- Founding of *Francofonds*. - Founding of the parish Kateri Tekakwitha in Winnipeg; the first Aboriginal parish in the city of Winnipeg.
1979		- The Official Language Act of 1890 is declared unconstitutional. - Invention of the compact disc (CD).
1980	Diocesan sponsorship project: 40 parishes welcome refugees from Laos, Vietnam and Cambodia.	Unveiling of Franco-Manitoban flag.
1982		Adoption of the Canadian Charter of Rights and Freedoms. Article 23 of the Charter guarantees official-language minority groups the right to access and administer schools in their mother tongue.
1983	Start of the Vietnamese and Laotian Catholic communities.	Sixth Assembly of the World Council of Churches in Vancouver.
1984	Renew Program in the parishes. This three-year program was followed by small group meetings.	Pope John Paul II visits Manitoba.
1985		The Supreme Court of Canada declares that all laws in the province of Manitoba are unconstitutional.
1987-88		*États généraux* of the Manitoban Francophonie. 
1988	- Launch of Nathanael, faith-based education program for adults. - Mgr Maurice Baudoux dies on July 1st.	
1989		Invention of the World Wide Web.
1990	Implementation of the *Commission diocésaine de catéchèse* by Mgr Hacault to clearly express the goals of the educational program in the French schools.	
1991	Diocesan sponsorship of refugees continues: camps in Thailand close and Saint Boniface welcomes new refugees.	Inauguration of CKXL, the community radio station of Manitoba.
1992	Opening of the Catholic School of Evangelization. A lay ministry that focuses on living the Gospel in community and proclaiming it through the ministry of evangelization.	The Government of Canada acknowledges the unique and historic role played by Louis Riel as founder of Manitoba.
1993	Participation of young pilgrims in World Youth Day (WYD) in Denver, U.S.A.	Adoption of Bill 34 – This education law enacts the creation of a French-language school division to open in the fall of 1994.
1997-00	Preparation of the Great Jubilee for the Year 2000.	
2000	- Mgr Antoine Hacault dies on April 13th at the age of 74. - Participation of young pilgrims in WYD in Rome.	

1974 to 2000 – Era of Mgr Antoine Hacault. Period of continued renewal on the wave of Vatican II: Presbyteral Council, parish pastoral councils, training and involvement of laypeople, youth movements, family pastoral services.
Founding of 3 parishes and canonical erection of 5 parishes.

DATE	ARCHDIOCESE OF SAINT BONIFACE	MANITOBA, CANADA, THE WORLD AND THE CHURCH
2001	 - **Consecration of Mgr Émilius Goulet, P.S.S., 7th bishop and 6th archbishop of Saint Boniface,** September 16th.	September 11th – Terrorist attacks in the United States: in New York, on the Pentagon in Washington and in Pennsylvania.
2001-09	- Follow-up to the Great Jubilee of the Year 2000: The New Evangelization.	
2001-2015	- The diocesan refugee sponsorship committee, first organized in the 1990s, remains active: refugees are welcomed from Ethiopia, Eritrea, Central Africa, Central America, Somalia, Sudan and Afghanistan.	
2002	Arrival of the Congrégation des Joséphites.	
2003		Creation of *Accueil francophone* to help French-speaking newcomers settle in Manitoba.
2005	- *Ad limina* visit to Rome – Mgr Goulet presents pastoral priorities in his diocese: youth pastoral services, Catholic schools, vocations, Liturgy, ecumenism. - Arrival of the community The Daughters of Wisdom. - Participation of more than 80 young pilgrims in WYD in Cologne.	
2006	Arrival of the community Handmaids of the Holy Child Jesus.	
2009	Mgr Émilius Goulet retires at the age of 75.	

2001 to 2009 – Era of Mgr Émilius Goulet. This period, which followed the Great Jubilee of the Year 2000, is focused on the New Evangelization. Canonical erection of 3 parishes.

DATE	ARCHDIOCESE OF SAINT BONIFACE	MANITOBA, CANADA, THE WORLD AND THE CHURCH
2009	**-Mgr Albert LeGatt is named 8th bishop and 7th archbishop of Saint Boniface on July 3rd.**  - Implementation of a pastoral plan.	

DATE	ARCHDIOCESE OF SAINT BONIFACE	MANITOBA, CANADA, THE WORLD AND THE CHURCH
2011	Launch of model ARISE Together in Christ. (2011 to 2014).	CUSB becomes *Université de Saint-Boniface* (USB).
2013	- Launch of 2013-2018 Action Plan – Spiritual and Pastoral Renewal of the Archdiocese of Saint Boniface. - Launch of a catechetical policy.	*États généraux* of the Manitoban Francophonie 2013-2016.
2015	Organization of a diocesan social justice committee.	
2015-16	Sponsorship of refugees from Iraq, Syria and Libya.	Wave of immigrants at the Canadian-American border escaping the United States after the presidential election of Donald Trump.
2016	- Arrival of the community Sons of Mother of Mercy. - Arrival of the community Sons of St. Eugene de Mazenod. - Inauguration and benediction of the Saint Boniface Heritage Garden in 2016 and the Reconciliation and Peace Garden in 2018.	
2017	- Launch of Alpha, a series of interactive sessions exploring the basics of the Christian faith. - Arrival of the Society of African Missions.	The SFM changes its name from *Société franco-manitobaine* to *Société de la francophonie manitobaine*.
2018	Synod – Youth and Faith.	

2009 to present – Era of Mgr LeGatt. Period of new pastoral initiatives that promote evangelization and adult faith-based education; period of reconciliation with Aboriginal peoples; period of refugee sponsorship and welcoming newcomers from various countries around the world. Canonical erection of 3 parishes.

Research: Jeannette R. Martin

Bibliography:

- Manitoba Education, Division du Bureau de l'éducation française, *Histoire du Canada 11e année*, programme d'études: document de mise en œuvre: programme français, 2012, Winnipeg, Manitoba.
- Website of the Saint Boniface Cathedral Parish *www.cathedralestboniface.ca*
- Website of the Archdiocese of Saint Boniface *http://www.archsaintboniface.ca/index.html?lang=en*
- Website of the Société Historique de Saint-Boniface *http://shsb.mb.ca/au_pays_de_riel* Histoire chronologique du diocèse de Saint-Boniface; Histoire chronologique des relations entre les autochtones et les autres populations; Histoire chronologique du Manitoba français. *http://archivesshsb.mb.ca/fr/list?q=photos&p=1&ps=20*
- Website of the Ministry of Education of Saskatchewan (2000), Social sciences 30, Canadian studies, Program of study. https://www.k12.gov.sk.ca/docs/francais/schumaines/second/chrono3.html

Acknowledgements:

Gilles Lesage, Director, Société Historique de Saint-Boniface; *Laura Gosselin*, *S.N.J.M.*, Archivist; *Jeannine Sorin*, Administrative Assistant, Chancery of the Archdiocese of Saint Boniface; *Jean-Marie Taillefer*, Historian; *Diane Bélanger*, Coordinator of Catechesis and *Nathanael*, Francophone Sector, Archdiocese of Saint Boniface; *Karen Loeb*, Translator.